INDIAN INTERNET
Copyright Law

INDIAN INTERNET
Copyright Law

with special reference to author's
right in the digital world.

ABIDHA BEEGUM V.S.

PARTRIDGE

A Penguin Random House Company

Copyright © 2014 by ABIDHA BEEGUM V.S.

| ISBN: | Softcover | 978-1-4828-3873-2 |
| | eBook | 978-1-4828-3872-5 |

To order additional copies of this book, contact
Partridge India
000 800 10062 62
orders.india@partridgepublishing.com

www.partridgepublishing.com/india

Contents

*Dedicated to the Internet Authors
And Netizens.*

PREFACE

I have been a student of Intellectual Property Rights and at the time of preparation of a book, immediately it comes to my mind that whatever I have done in my studies will help me to make it successful. As it is my first effort, kindly forgive me in the shortcomings and intimate me about any kinds of suggestion for properly updating this humble work.

I always preferred to write a book on Internet copyright law which is a comparative analysis to the U.S. Digital Millennium Copyright Act and other legal systems because, Indian internet authors is getting minimal protection compared to other nations. A proper law to address the grievance of internet authors nowadays in the digital world is very essential.

Publishing work on the internet has became very common. It is the easiest way of making the work the work available to a worldwide audience. Along with the case of making the work available to the public with the help of internet, copy those work has become easier. It is quite possible that the author may permit the user to download, but may not permit further distribution or posting on the internet through some other website. Therefore in this study it become very difficult to search for liability and establish jurisdiction upon the entity that can be made responsible for online copyright infringement. The liability of internet service providers also is an important concern here. However the copyright law in India and the information Technology Act is not sufficient to meet the challenges posed by internet.

On the international level, several attempts have been made to deal with these issues. WIPO Copyright Treaty And European Union Directives in this regard provides for certain measures to address this problems. Moreover, the Specific Legislation On Intermediary Liability, in disseminating third-party content has been recognized and applied in many national laws, many of which related to criminal law. Even so, some of these laws have inspired national and international legislators in dealing with the issue of online liability for copyright infringement. Therefore, the Online Copyright Infringement Liability Limitation Act, 1998 which is a part of U.S. Copyright specific legislation, can be considered as a model legislation in this area.

Moreover, without expressing my sincere thanks to those who encouraged and helped me in completing this work, this task cannot be fulfilled.

First of all, I thank almighty for his love and care bestowed on me to complete my study and this work.

I express my sincere thanks to Dr. Elizebeth Verkey, Lecturer, School of Indian Legal Thought, for her valuable guidance and meticulous support for the academic improvement and successful completion of this work.

I place on record my deep and sincere gratitude to my husband, my in laws and my family members for their affectionate blessings and supports throughout my life. Finally, I extend my thanks to my friends who have made critical comments and valuable suggestions.

Abidha Beegum.V.S.,

Chapterisation

The first chapter so far gave brief overview of the copyright justification and implications of digital media along with burning issues regarding the online copyright protection.

The second chapter deals with the exclusive statutory rights of the Author of a work Internet.

The third chapter of this study deals with the basic Internet challenges relating to author's rights and the necessity of copyright protection to be made available in the Internet.

The fourth chapter handling the theories of liability for infringement of author's right in internet. This chapter is progressing through many case laws regarding direct, contributory and vicarious liability of service providers.

The fifth chapter deal with limitations on copyright owner's exclusive rights and the remedies available to protect the interest of the authors.

The sixth chapter deals with the moral right aspects in the internet and author's right and last chapter conclude the study with certain recommendations.

TABLE OF ABBREVIATIONS

ABB   -   Bulletin Board Service
CD   -   Compact Disc
CDPA   -   Copyright Designs and patent Act
CGI   -   Common Gateway Interface
DMCA   -   Digital Millennium Copyright Act
DRM   -   Digital Right Management
ECD   -   European Copyright Directive
EU   -   European Union
HTML   -   Hypertext Markup Language
ISP   -   Internet Service Providers
IT   -   Information Technology
LAN   -   Local Area Network
OCILLA   -   Online Copyright Infringement liability
               Limitations Act
OSP   -   Online service providers
P2P   -   Peer to Peer
RAM   -   Random Access Memory
RIAA   -   Recording Industry Association of America
ROM   -   Read Only Memory
TEACH   -   Technology Education and Intellectual
               Property Rights

UK	-	United Kingdom
URL	-	Uniform Resource Locator
US	-	United States
WCT	-	WIPO Copyright Treaty

Table of Cases

1. Reno v. ACLU, 1107 S.C.1997, 1239.
2. R. G. Anand v. Deluxe films AIR 1978, S.C.., 1613.
3. Wham -O-Manufacturing Co. v. Lincoln Industries, 1982 RPC.
4. Shyam Shah v. Gaya Prasad Gupta, AIR 1971 ALL 192.
5. Manfstaengal v. Empire palace (1894)3 Ch.
6. Sega Enterprises v. MAPHIA, 948 F.Supp. 679, N.D.California 1996.
7. RIAA v. Napster, 114 F.Supp 2d 896, N.D.California 2000.
8. Advanced Computer Services v. MAI System, F.Supp. 356.E.D.Va 1994.
9. MAI System Corp. v. Peak Computer Inc. 991.F.2d 5119th Circuit, 1993.
10. Religious Technology Center v. Netcom Online Communication Services, 907 F.Supp. N.D.California, 1995.
11. Playboy Enterprises Inc. v. Frena 839. F.Supp. 648 N.D.California, 1996.
12. Shea v. Reno, 930 F.Supp. 916

13. Ticketmaster Corp. v. Tickets.com. Inc, 54 U.S.P.Q.2d.1344, C.D.California, 2000.

14. Sony Corp. of America v. Universal City Studio, Inc. 464 U.S.1984.

15. Marobie. FL. Inc. v. National Association of Fire Equipment Distributors, 983. F.Supp. N.D.111, 1997.

16. Ticketmaster v. Microsoft, U.S. Code No. 97-3055, DP, 1997.

17. E-bay Inc. v. Bidder's Edge Inc. No -922/2000, RMW, N.D.California, 2000.

18. CBS Songs v. Amstrad, 1988, A.C, 1058.

19. Intellectual Reserve, Inc. v. Utah Lighthouse Ministry Inc., 75 F. Supp 2d, 1290, 1999.

20. Bernstein. v. J. C. Penney Inc. 1998 U.S. Dist. Lexis 19048 C.D. California, 1998.

21. Shetland Times v. Dr. Jonathan Wills(1997)F.S.R.

22. Arrista Records, Inc. v. MP3 Board Inc. U.S. Dist LEXIS 16165, 2002.

23. Leslie A. Kelley v. Arriba Soft Corp. 280, F.3d, 9th circuit, 2002.

24. Mirage Editions Inc. v. Albuquerque, A.R.T. Co., 856, F.2.d.9th circuit, 1988.

25. Lee v. A.R.T. Co., 964, F.2d., 965, 7th circuit, 1992.

26. Lewis Galoob Toys Inc. v. Nintendo Inc., 964, F.2d., 9th circuit, 1995.

27. Microstar v. Forgmen, 154, F. 3d, 9th circuit, 1998.

28. Washington Post Co. v. Total News Inc., 97 civ, 1990, SDNY, Feb.20, 1997.

29. Journal Gazette Co. v. Midwest Internet Exchange, 98 cv.0130, N.D. Indiana.

30. Future dontics, Inc. v. Applied Anagaramatics Inc. 45 U.S.P.Q.2d, 2005, C.D.California, 1998.

31. National Football League v. TV Radio Corp.53 U.S.P.Q.2d, 2000.

32. In re Gator Corp. Software and Copyright Litigation, 259 F.Supp. 2d 1378, J.P.M.L.2003.

33. Wells Fargo and Co. Case, 293 F. Supp 2d, 747.

34. A & M Records Inc. v. Napster Inc., 239 F. Supp 3d 1004.

35. Costar Group Inc. v. Loopnet Inc., 164 F.Supp. 2d, 1051, C.D. California, 2002.

36. RIAA v. Verizon Internet Services, 351, F.3d. 1229.

37. ALS Scan Inc. v Remar Q Cmtys Inc.239, F.3d, 619.

38. Hendrikson v. eBay Inc.165, F.Supp. 2d, 1082.

39. Perfect 10 Inc. v. Cybernet Ventures Inc., 213, F. Supp 2d, C.D. California, 2002.

40. Re Aimster Copyright Litigation, 334, F.3d, 7th circuit, 2003.

41. Ellison v. Robertson, 189, F.Supp. 2d, 1051.

42. Rossi v. Motion Picture Association of America, U.P.S.Q. 2d, 1047.

43. Ladbroke(Football) Ltd v. William Hill(Football) Ltd., 1964, I, All. E.R, 465.

44. Escorts construction Equipment Ltd v. Action Construction Equipment Ltd. AIR, 1999, Del, 73.

45. Atari Games Corp. v. Nintendo of America Inc., 975, F.2d, 840.

46. Apple Computer v. Formula International, 594, F.Supp, 617.

47. RIAA v. Diamond Multimedia Systems, 180 F.3d, 1999.

48. Trial Systems v. Southeaster Express Co.64, F.3d, 9th circuit, 1995.

49. Garware Plastic v. Telelink, AIR, 1989, Bom. 331.

50. Maganlal savani v. Rupan Pictures AIR, 2000, Bom.416.

51. Prince Albert v. Strange, 41 E.R.1171.

52. Hotaling v. Church of Jesus Christ of Latter -Day Saints, 118, F.3d, 199, 4th circuit, 1997.

53. Michaels v. Internet Entert. Group Inc., 5F. Supp 2d, 823, C.D. California, 1998.

54. Columbia Pictures Ind. v. Aveco Inc., 800 F.2d, 3rd circuit, 1986.

55. Midway Mfg. Co, v. Artic International, 704 F.2d, 965.

56. Sid and Marty Kroft Television Productions v. Mc Donald's Corp.562 F.2d, 9th circuit, 1977.

57. Costello Publications Co. v. Rostelle, 70 F.2d, D.C. circuit, 1981.

58. Sega Enterprises Ltd. v. Sebella, 948 F.Supp., 648, N.D.California, 1996.

59. Playboy Enterprises v. Webbworld, 968 F.Supp. 1171, N.D. Texas, 1997.

60. Playboy Enterprises v. Russ Hardenburgh 982 F.Supp. N.D. Ohio 1997.

61. Playboy Enterprises v. Sanfilippo, 1998 U.S. Dist. LEXIS. 5125, S.D. California, 1998.

62. Los Angels Times v. Free Republic 54 U.S.P.Q. 2d.1543, C.D. California, 2000.

63. MP3.Com Inc. v. UMG recordings Inc. No.DD Civ. 0472, SDNY, jan.21, 2000.

64. Cable/Home Communication Corp. v. Network Production Inc., 902 F.2d 11th circuit, 1990.

65. Casella v. Morris, 820.F.2d 11th circuit, 1987.

66. Fronovisa Inc. v. Cherry Auction Inc. 76F.3d, 9th circuit, 1996.

67. MGM Studios Inc. v. Grokster Ltd., 125 S ct, 2005.

68. Shapiro Bernstein and Co. v. H.L Green Co. 326F. 2d, Second circuit, 1963.

69. Cubby v. Compuserve, 776, F.Supp. (SDNY 1999).

70. Screen Gems –Columbia Music Inc. v. Mark P. Records Inc., 256 F. Supp, (SDNY 1966).

71. Gershwin Publishing Corp. v. Columbia Artists Management Inc., 443, F.2d, 2nd circuit, 1971.

72. CCH Canadian v. Law Society of upper Canada, 2004, SCC, 13.

73. Shetland Times v. Dr Jonathan Wills, 1997, FSR, 304.

74. Cable/Home Communication Corp. v. Network Production Inc.902, F.2d, 829.

75. L.A. Times v. Free Republic, 54 U.S.P.Q.2d.1453,

76. Kelly v. Arriba Soft Corp. 77, F.Supp 2d., 1116, C.D. California, 1998., 1999.

77. Marcus v. Rowley, 695, F.2d, 9th circuit, 1983.

78. Harper and Row Publishers Inc. v. Nation Enter. 471, U.S.1985.

79. American Geophysical Union v. Texaco Inc., 37, 3d, 2nd circuit, 1994.

80. Anton Piller v. Manufacturing Process Ltd. 1967 Ch.55.

81. Gates v. Swift, 1981.FSR, 57.

82. Systematic Ltd v. London Computer Center Ltd., 1983, FSR, 313.

83. Columbia Picture Ind. v. Robinson, 1986, FSR, 367.

84. Raindrop Date System Ltd v. Systematic Ltd., 1988, FSR, 354.

85. Leisure Data System Ltd v. Bell, 1988, FSR, 367.

86. Redwood Music Ltd v. Chappell and Co. Ltd, 1982, RPC, 109.

87. A. K. Mukherjee v. State,(1994)54, DLT, 461.

88. Manu Bhandari v. Kala Vikas Pictures, AIR, 1987, Del., 13.

89. Moore v. Daily News Plc. 1972, L. Q.B, 441.

90. K.P.M. Sundaram v. Ratton Prakashan Mandir and Other, AIR, 1983, Del., 461.

91. Wilay Eastern Ltd v. Indian Institute of Management, 58,(1995), DLT, 449.

92. Amar Nath Sengal v. Union of India, 2002, (25)PTC, 56, Delhi.

93. University of London Press v. University of Tutorial Press, 1916(2), Ch., 601.

TABLE OF STATUTES AND DIRECTIVES

1. European Database Directive, 1996.
2. Computer Programmes Directive, 1991.
3. European Copyright Directive, 2001.
4. European Electronic Commerce Directive, 2001.
5. WIPO Copyright Treaty, 1996.
6. Copyright Designs and patent Act, 1988.
7. Digital Millennium Copyright Act, 1998.
8. Digital Performance Right in Sound Recording Act, 1995.
9. Indain Copyright Act, 1957
10. Indain Copyright (Amendment)Act, 1994.
11. Indain Copyright (Amendment)Act, 1999.
12. United States Copyright Act, 1976.
13. Singapore Copyright Amendment Act, 1999.
14. Technology, Education and Copyright Harmonisation Act, 2001.
15. Belgium Copyright Act, 1994.
16. Berne Convention, 1971.
17. Berne Convention, Implementation Act, 1988.
18. South Africa Copyright Act, 1988.
19. New Zealand Copyright Act, 1798.
20. Australian Copyright Amendment (Moral Rights) Act, 2002.

21. Universal Declaration of Human Rights.
22. French Civil Code.
23. Information Technology Act, 2000.
24. TRIPS Agreement, 1995.

Chapter 1

Introduction

An author's exclusive right to control the making of copies of original work is the fundamental basis of the copyright regime. The technological development in printing, have introduced new ways and methods of producing and distributing information in various format and Internet is the lasted explosion in this digital context. Therefore Internet and copyright is treated as one of the most inflamed issue in the current Intellectual property regime[1]. Probably the most difficult challenge to legislators and courts is that, regulating the use and abuse of copyright material accessed through Internet.

---

[1] W.R.Cornish & Llewlyn, Intellectual property; Patents. copyright, Trademark, Designs, VthEd, sweet&Maxwell, London, 2003, p.795

ABIDHA BEEGUM V.S.

From Analogue to Digital-
Copyright Implications

In contrast to traditional 'analog' methods of recording works, digitization converts all words, images, sounds and graphics etc. into binary numbers, that is either ones or zeros. These digitally stored works are then transferred over the networks which is available to the public for their appropriate uses. Here also, the balancing of conflicting public and private interest should be maintained. One of the existing belief is that any work which is available in internet express a tacit consent of some sort by the creator of such works in its copying, reproduction or transmission. Thus digital technology enables the transmission and use of all of this protected materials in digital form over interactive network.

Need for Protection

Justification for providing copyright protection to authors can be generally considered to be four fold. According to Natural Law Philosophy, every man has a natural right over the result of his labor and so the author who has put in effort to produce the work shall have a right to enjoy the fruits of his labour. Another theory is that such protection acts as a just reward for the skill and labour of the author, who deserves to be remunerated when his work is exploited. Moreover, if such investments is rewarded, it stimulates the creativity of the author[2].

---

[2]   Peter Drahos, A Philosophy of intellectual properties Dartmouth publications, Aldershort, 1996.p.136

It is in the interest of the society, that the author should be encouraged to create more, as well as publish their works, since new works are additions to the cultural stock of the society. Thus the law of copyright provides incentive to the creative effort and to the creation and dissemination of works to the benefit of the society as a whole[3]. But in this new information area, internet has been described as the world's biggest copy machine. It permit to press easily large quantity of information at a comparatively less time and less cost method[4]. Therefore it is necessary to adjust the legal system with the interest of the author of a work in Internet, by recognizing the importance of their contribution and should give them reasonable control over the exploitation of their work to make profit from it.

Accordingly, the goal of policy makers has been to achieve an appropriate balance through law, by providing strong and effective rights. But it should be within reasonable limits and with fair exceptions for the development of science, culture and the economy. If right holders are secure in their right ability to sell and license their property over the Internet, they will exploit their right fully and make more and valuable works available through this medium.

Therefore it is necessary to introduce, the categories of people who may be involved in the internet activities and liable for violation of the rights of copyright owners. They are users, website authors and service providers.

Service providers include Internet service providers and bulletin board services. Internet service providers only provide

---

3   S.M. Stewart, International Copyright & Neighboring Rights, London, Butterworths, 1989.p.13-23

4   L.Lessing, The lawof horse:What cyber law Might teach, Harvard Law Review, Jan.2001

access to the Internet. Their services are widely used all over the world and this establishes extensive liability. Whereas online service providers provide access to extensive content along with Internet access[5]. It is a concept broader than internet services typically provide access to content and forums, but no Internet access.

Basic Issues regarding Internet & Author's Right

The most fundamental issue raised for the fields of copyright and related rights is the determination of the scope of protection in the digital environment, how rights are defined and what exceptions and limitations are permitted. Other important issues include how rights are enforced and administered in this environment, who is in the chain of dissemination of infringing material, can be held liable for the infringement and the questions of jurisdiction and applicable law. Moreover what all activities constitute infringement of author's right in internet and is there any extension of moral right to the Internet author?

Internet is a major global pipeline where the selling and delivery of creative content and information takes place, which is easily accessible and can be got within seconds by just a simple click of the mouse. Various activities are at present possible through Internet beyond the territorial limits[6]. Copyright Law deal with the creation, distribution and sale of the protected works in the form of tangible copies, but it is difficult to

---

[5]   OCILLA, 1998, Sec.512(k)(1)

[6]   Patrick E.cole, Buissiness-The internet Economy, Time, July20, 1998, p.34

identify the location of the copy of the storage, identification and distribution of literary, artistic and audio –visual material held in digital format[7]. Many transactions as we know today reflect some transmission of copyrighted works on line, which may allegedly infringed the rights of the author's of such copyrighted work. Therefore a detailed consideration over all the issue is necessary to protect the interest of the authors.

The owners of copyrights and related rights are granted with a range of different rights to control or be remunerated for various types of uses of their property. The development of digital technologies, permitting transmission of works over networks, has raised questions about how these rights apply in the new environment. When multiple copies of works are transmitted through networks, is the reproduction rights implicated by each copy? Is there a communication to the public when a work is not broadcast, and simply made available to individual members of the public if and when they wish to see or hear it? Moreover, does a public performance takes place when a work is viewed at different times by different individuals on their personal computers or other digital devices?

In general, anyone who violates the exclusive rights of a copyright owner infringes the copyright. In the field of Internet also, the situation is the same. Therefore it is necessary to analyze, what are the instances of copyright infringement and the modes of infringement and the modes of infringement in the Internet. And is there any protected activities which are exempted from such infringement should also have to look

---

[7]   W.R.Cornish & M. Llewelyn, Intellectual property; Patents, Copyright, Trademark, designs, Vth Edn, Sweet 7 Maxwell, London, 2003, p.795

into for the purpose of verification of author's right and the enforcement of such rights.

There are issue regarding exception and limitation to copyright. Can these exceptions and limitations intended to the analogue media extended to the digital media and is it too broad or too narrow? Some exceptions, if applied literally in the digital environment can eliminate large sectors of existing market but others may implement public policy goals, but be written too respectively to apply to network transmissions. Is there any chance for new exceptions in the new circumstances? These questions must be examined in the light of the general standard established in treaties for the permissibility of exceptions, to certain rights. It is known as a three-step test. That is, exceptions are permitted "in certain special cases" that "do not conflict with a normal exploitation" of the work and "do not unreasonably prejudice the legitimate interest of the owner[8] ".How does this standard apply in the digital environment?

Issue of enforcement and licensing is another concern when works are exploited on digital network. For a meaningful legal protection, right holders must be able to detect and stop the dissemination of unauthorized digital copies.

By the very nature of digital networks, another issue is that, when a work transmitted from one point to another, or made available for the public for access, numerous parties are involved in the transmission. This includes users and

---

[8]   Berne Convention, 1971, Art.9(2);TRIPS Agreement, 1995, art.13.

entities that provide Internet access or online services[9]. When such service providers participate in transmission or making available materials which infringe copyright, are they liable for the infringement? Such liability may arise in two circumstances. That is, like the service provider itself is found to have engaged in unauthorized acts of reproduction or communication to the public and if it is held responsible for contributing to the act of infringement by another.

Under these situation, the immediate concern is on the potential liability of online service and access providers for infringements taking place through their services. The question is that, can service providers be held legally responsible for the unauthorized exercise of the rights of copyright owners by individual using their services. There is only one provision in India concerning this issue[10]. Under the laws of many countries, the answer is depending upon the circumstances of each case[11].

The liability issue has significant International implications due to the borderless nature of Internet as the medium. Depends on the particular circumstances and legal traditions in each country, approach to this liability may be different.

Even thought the TRIPS Agreement dealt with enforcement of rights, the issue of protecting digital materials were not addressed. Though there is the possibility to interpret Berne Convention[12] while dealing with reproduction right in the digital environment, there was considerable opposition having regard to the background in which the Article was

---

[9]   OCILLA, 1998, Sec.512(k)(1)
[10]   Information Technology Act, 2000, Sec.79.
[11]   OCILLA, 1998, Sec.512(1)
[12]   Berne Convention, 1971, Art.9

introduced in Berne. There is also no provision in this Convention which is capable of interpretation that can afford protection to the communication to public or publication right author in digital context.

In 1996, the Diplomatic Conference at Geneva adopted the WIPO Copyright Treaty. The ultimate result was that the treaty is neutral with the issue of liability regarding the activities of service providers. However, in an Agreed Statement to the WLT, there is one reference to this issue[13]. In response to the digital technology and Internet, this treaty constitutes the first update of the Berne Convention. The treaty agreed to extend article 9 of the Berne to digital environment and expressly stated that storage of works in digital form would constitute reproduction[14]. The Treaty agreed that, all the exceptions and limitations recognized under the Berne would be applicable to digital material as well. To protect the interest of the owners of copyright, this gives freedom to nations to introduce appropriate provisions in their domestic Law[15]. More over European Union copyright Directive, 2001 and European Commerce Directive, 2001 are there to address certain issue with reference to activities of service providers. Therefore the International initiatives in this matter are an important consideration here.

Moreover, in the United States of America, the congress has enacted copyright- specific legislation as part of the Digital Millennium Copyright Act, 1998 regarding the liability of service providers[16]. This is known as by the name Online

---

[13] WCT, 1996, Art.8.

[14] Ibid, Art.1(4)

[15] Ibid, Art.10.

[16] OCILLA, 1998, Sec.512

Copyright Infringement Liability Limitation Act. The Act adds a new section 512 to chapter 5 of the United States Copyright Act, which deals with the enforcement of copyrights.

It is by this time a-well -known formula that we should understand that, we live in an age which is undergoing a swift technological and social change. Technologies and business that were unknown a few years ago are now pervasive. Most recently, the explosive growth of telecommunications technology, sometimes referred to as the Global Information Infrastructure or The Information Super high way which includes the Internet, has enabled people to be in through the Internet is still there to be regularized by the Legislators. We have still a long road ahead of us so as to reach the destination for finding out a possible and trustworthy solutions for the copyright protection and author's right when it comes to the vast arena of Internet.

CHAPTER II

Exclusive Statutory Rights of A Copyright Owner in Internet

> Authors of literary and artistic works............shall
> have the exclusive right of authorizing reproduction
> of these work in any manner or form[17].

The development of copyright law has always been in response to challenges raised by new technologies, such as the original printing press, that enable the reproduction and distribution of works. In this regard, the Internet, or any digital network for that matter, presents some very difficult challenges. Digital networks result in many automatic copies. Routers make temporary copies of data packets for timing and alignment purposes. Cache servers make complete copies of works in order to place them in physical locations closer to users in order t o improve the speed and efficiency of the networks. Browsing software and personal computers make copies of works that are downloaded from the Network and displayed by the computer.

---

[17]   Berne convention, 1971, Art.9(1)

Users also make copies. There copies can then be distributed around the world in a moments at almost no cost, potentially creating exponential losses for copyright owners.

INTERNET & AUTHORS RIGHT

Every time a new technology that had an impact on the reproduction, distribution and transmission of works protected under copyright was invented, the work fought to ensure maximum protection of their rights[18]. One of the objective of copyright law is to promote individual Interest. This involved incentive to the authors to encourage creation of new work. Recognition of the authorship of the work and ensuring economic returns through the copyright law is intended to achieve this[19]. The author is expected to commercially exploit this bundle of rights with the help of industrialists. The individual interest also promotes incentive for investment in the production and distribution of the work to the public. Copyright law also aims at achieving public interest of access to the works at reasonable cost. Thus the major function of a copyright law is to ensure a proper balance between these conflicting interests[20].

To protect the economic interest of the author, law recognizes a bundle of rights that can be exclusively enjoyed by the author. These rights include the right of reproduction,

---

[18] Ronald V. Belting, Copyrights Culture. The political economy of intellectual property, West view press, 1996.

[19] Peter Drahos, A philosophy of Intellectual properties, Dartmouth publications, Aldershot, 1996, p.136

[20] Gillan Davies, Copyright and public Interest, Maxplanc institute, 1994

distribution, communication of the work to public, adaptation of the work etc[21]. The traditional interpretation of this right in the context of existing technology is a necessity to protect the interest of the authors and owners in Internet.

Right to reproduce the work

The right of reproduction is considered by the European commission[22], as the core of copyright. Reproduction means reproducing the original exactly or copying a substantial part of the original work[23]. The owner of copyright reserves the right of reproduction and hence any person, who reproduces the work without the owner's permission infringes the owner's reproduction right[24].

In the digital networked environment, copies are no more than haphazard manifestations of works being transmitted in immaterial form over wired or wireless channels[25]. However with regard to the test of substantial similarity on the Internet, there arises no difficulty as the work, if copied, will be similar and identical to that of the original author. Hence in an interesting case[26], it was held that "even the works that

---

[21] Indian copyright Act, 1957, Sec.14

[22] Commission of the European Communities, Green paper, Copyright and related right in the information society, Brussels, July 29, 1995, p.49

[23] Ladbroke (Football) Ltd. v. William Hill (Football) Ltd 1964 All.E.R.465

[24] Escorts construction Equipment ltd v. Action Construction Equipment Ltd. ALL E.R.465

[25] Edberg J. Dommering, Copyright being washed away through Electronic sieve, P. Bernt Hughenhottz Edn.1996.p.7

[26] Atari games Corp. v. Nintedo of America Inc., 975 F 2d, 840

warrant limited copyright protection, verbatim copying is an infringement".

According to Kohler, technical criteria should not determine the scope of reproduction right[27]. Copyright protect against acts of unauthorized communication, not consumptive usage. The interpretation of the reproduction right should not be made dependant on technical coincidence[28]. The right of reproduction covers any copy suitable for communicative purposes[29]. Even so, the more reception or consumption of information by end users has traditionally remained outside the scope of Copyright monopoly[30].

Copyright infringement in the online environment often involves a violation of the reproduction right that occurs by transferring data form one computer to another. In a striking case[31], it was held that copies stored in random access memory (RAM) were temporary and running a computer program from RAM does not create an Infringed copy.

However, in another case[32], software was downloaded into RAM when the defendant turns the computer on in the course of performing maintenance. In doing so, the defendant was able to view the software program to assist him in diagnosing

[27] Joseph Kohler, Copyright related rights, Oxford, 1st Edition, 1980, p113.

[28] M. Lehmann, Copyright and computer programs, Sweets And Maxwell, 2nd Edition, 1993, p.12

[29] P.B. Hugerholts, Convergence and Divergence of Intellectual property law; The case of the Software Directive, Jan.Kabel, 2nd Edition, 1998p.323

[30] P.F. Noleen, Copies in Copyright, RIDA, 1980.p.113

[31] Apple Computer v. Formula International, 594 F.Supp. 617.

[32] MAI System Corp. Peak Computer, Inc 1991, F 2nd 511.(9th Cir.1993)

the problem. The court found that the copy create in RAM was sufficiently permanent and "fixed" to satisfy the copyrights law and cases of infringement. Hence, unauthorized downloading of software in to RAM and using it for personal gain constitute both "copying" and infringement.

Other instances of an unauthorized reproduction and copyright infringement are "scanning" a copyrighted printed document in to a digital file and uploading or downloading a digital copyrighted file to a bulletin board system.

Client caching merely facilitates consumptive usage. The temporary reproduction made in the client's RAM or hard disk have no other purposes that to facilitate browsing or viewing the work. The dissemination enhancing rationale of copyright presents an even stronger argument against automatically equating proxy caching[33] with reproduction right. It is true that, the Internet of the present and foreseeable future, would collapse if no caching were allowed. Treating caching as a restricted activity would be wholly irrational[34]. Then the question is that whether or not proxy caching is exempted[35] from liability. The Betamax case[36], and its progeny suggest

---

[33] Proxy catching generally takes place at the sever level. In this, a copy of material requested by users gets stored on a server other than the users server. Generally the 1st stores, on its own servers, web pages that have been requested by its users.

[34] Chris barles, For an Introduction of Art of catching, DIPPER, September 30, 1999.p.1-2

[35] Trotter Hardy, Computer RAM Copies; A Hit Or a Myth? Historical perspective on caching as microcosm of current copyright concerns; Dayton Law Review, 1997, p.423

[36] Sony Corporation Of America v. Universal City Studios, 464 U.S.417, 1984.

that client caching, is a fair use. The Rio decision[37] projecting the use of portable digital music recorders for downloading MP3 file from the Internet. The court of Appeal for Ninth Circuit held that, the Rio merely makes copies in order to render portable or space shift those file that already reside on a user's hard drive. Such copying is paradigmatic non-commercial personal use and entirely consistent with the purpose of law. In an interesting case[38] the court held that temporary copying while browsing is the function equivalent of reading and hence dose not enter into the copyright Law. The process of temporary copying of the work on the RAM is somewhat similar to the act of a person going to a bookshop and just looking at a book[39]. Therefore it can be concluded that temporary copying on the RAM does not amount to copyright violation and should be treated as a technical necessity. It may also not be wrong to say that, the author who knows that such copying is obvious and incidental, has impliedly given the authority for such temporary copying.

Right of communication to the public

Communication to the public[40] means making any work available for being seen or heard or otherwise enjoyed by the public directly or by any means of display or diffusion other than

---

37   RIAA v. Diamond Multimedia systems, 180 F.3d. 1072, 1999
38   Religious Technology Center v. Netcom Online Communication Services, 907 F.Supp. 1361
39   Advanced Computer services v.MAI Sys, 845 F.Spp.356.(E.D. Va. 1994):Triad Sys. v. Southeaster Express Co.64 F.3d 1330(9th cir1995)
40   Indian Copyright Act, 1957, Sec.2(ff)

by issuing copies of such work. That means regardless of whether any member of the public actually sees, hears or otherwise enjoys the work so made available[41]. Communication through satellite, cable, or any other means of simultaneous communication etc. may include communication via Internet, within this ambit.

EU Directive on copyright and Related rights in the Information Society[42], seeks to protect digital on –demand transmission on the basis of harmonized right of communication to the public[43]. By this provision, authors and related right holders will have the right to authorize or prohibit any communication of their works or material to the public so that individual members of the public may access them from a place and at a time chosen by them[44]. However, to limit the massive potential for abuse of rights by the use of new technology, any exceptions or limitations to the exclusive right of the rights holder adopted by an E.U Member must satisfy the three step test set out under the Bern convention[45]. The test provides that any limitations imposed upon a right holders exclusive rights shall only apply;

a) In certain special cases.

b) Where they do not conflict with the normal exploitation of the work; and

c) Where to do so would reasonably prejudice the Legitimate interests of the rights holders.

---

[41] Garware Plastics v. Telelink, AIR 1989 Bom.331.

[42] ECD, 2001, Art. 3.

[43] Trever Black, Special Repot, Intellectual Property in the Digital Era, Sweet & Maxwell, London, 2002, p.9.

[44] ECD 2001, Art.3.

[45] Berne Convention, 1971, art.9(2)

Right of distribution

Copyright Law grants owner of copyright, the exclusive right to issue copies of the work to the public. Distribution amount to copyright infringement, if the copies of the particular work are distribution to the public without the prior permission of the copyright owner. But the making available of copies to a private group may not amount to the issuance of copies to the public[46].

Because a copyright is the exclusive property of the owner, the right to exercise interest, such as selling renting or leasing the copyright, is protected by the court[47]. A person who does not own the copyright and makes it available on a bulletin board service can be liable for copyright infringement.

With specific reference to the right of distribution to computers, no sooner has work been exhibited on the Internet, then the distribution right is said to be in effect. There appears to be a very thin line between distribution and display Hardly any distinction can be drawn between the two terms when the right is regulated in cyberspace.

Copyright infringement in computers takes place immediately if the distribution right is taken away from the copyright owner in these ways:-

a) The copyrighted work is distributed to various net users through electronic mail,

---

[46]   Prince Albert v.Strange, 41E.R.1171
[47]   Ferrera, Lichtenstein, Reder, Bird, Schiano, Cyber law Text & Cases, 2nd Ed. Thomson, 2003. p92

b) The copyrighted work is distributed to the public by taking print outs of the work and then physically distributing it and

c) The copyrighted work is distributed when the work is displayed on the Internet web pages.

To show distribution, it is not necessary to prove that others actually copied or used the work, only that the defendant knowingly made it available to the public[48]. Distribution occurs when all steps necessary to make a work available to the public at large. Thus the right of public distribution is equivalent to public display and it is violated no sooner than the work is displayed on the Internet.

In a case[49], the court held that, the actions of the defendant, of encouraging his subscriber to upload Sega Games to his BBS which he would then his subscribers to download through the Internet, amounted to violation of the plaintiff's copyright as he induced, caused and materially contributed to the infringement.

In a prominent case[50] the court held that when an unauthorized photographs of playboy Enterprises were downloaded to a bulletin exclusive right of distribution was infringed by customers of the defendant. The defendant, bulletin board operator has an obligation to monitor its system

---

[48] Hotaling v. Church of Jesus Christ of Latter_day saints, 118 F 3d 199 at p.203, 4th cir 1997.

[49] Sega Enterprises v. MAPHIA, 857 F Supp, 679.N.D California 1994.

[50] Playboy Enterprises Inc.v. Frena, 839 F.Supp. 1552, M.D. Fla 1993.

to ensure that copyrighted documents are not being displayed and "downloaded" by its customers.

The same rationale regarding the copyright owner's exclusive right of distribution applies to e-mail attached or forwarded without the permission of the copyright owner. The position in a case[51], is that unauthorized copies of the plaintiff's electronic clip art files were placed on the defended's web pages. The court held that this constituted an infringing distribution because the files were available for downloading by Internet users.

Right to Perform and Display Publicly the Copyright Work

There are very Limited provisions for violation of right of public performance on the Internet. The issue that generally arises is the violation of public display right[52].

Generally, the right of public Performance is provided only to original literary, dramatic, choreographic and musical works[53]. Public performance is the performance that occurs at a place open to the public. It also includes a semi public place or any place where a substantial number of persons outside of a normal circle of a family and its social acquaintances are gathered[54]. The public performance copyrighted work by

---

[51] Marobie_Fl. Inc. v. National Association of Fire Equipment Distributors., 983 F.Supp. 1167 N.D.111 1997

[52] In India public display right is included in the right to communication to the public. Indian Copyright Act, 1957, sec. 2(ff)

[53] Ibid, Sec.14

[54] U.S. Copyright Act, 1976, sec.101.

any person without the copyright owner's consent amounts to infringement of copyright[55].

The display of work on postings, WebPages or any component of the Internet through which any person can view the work can be regarded as public display. It is immaterial, in the case of display on the Internet, whether, any net has viewed such work or not. The moment it is posted on the Internet, it would fall within the purview of public display.

In an interesting case[56], the court held that making the photographs available on BBS was public display even through the display was limited to subscribers, and subscribers viewed the photographs from the BBS on demand. Thus, the material available on the Internet even to a number of people is a public display. Similarly in another case[57], the administrator of the web page of the defendant, NAFED, placed certain files on NAFED's web pages containing three volumes of copyrighted clip art of the plaintiff. The court ruled that the placement of files containing the clip art on the web pages constituted a direct violation of both the plaintiff's distribution right and public display right.

Court in another case[58] have held that making available videotapes over the Internet without authorization and posting Unauthorized copies of electronic clip art on web pages could

---

[55]   Indian Copyright Act, 957, sec.51

[56]   Play boy Enterprises Inc. v.Frena, 839 F.Supp. 1552;29 USPQ 2d(BNA) 1827 MD Fla 1993

[57]   Marobie_FL, Inc. v. National Association of Fire Equipment distributors, 983 FSupp. 1167.45 USPQ2d [BNA]1236 ND 111, 1997.

[58]   Michaels v. Internet Entert. Group, Inc., FSupp. 2d823 C.D.California 1998

violate the copyright owner's exclusive statutory right of public display.

In relation with public performances, the court held that, the defendant improperly authorized public performances by renting videotapes and allowed customers to see the tapes in viewing rooms[59].

Thus it can be concluded that unauthorized display and public performance of copyrighted material on the Internet would amount to copyright infringement.

Adaptation[60] on the Internet

An alternation in the original work to produce a new work is generally termed as adaptation. Many countries protect the adaptation right of the copyright owner. However, there exists a difficulty in protection of adaptation right on the Internet due to the vastness and depth of the material available on the Internet.

There are many softwares and other copyrighted works which are freely available on the Internet for the user to use. But it is generally seen that users gather the works available on the Internet and add new features to it for commercial use.

Many cases have arisen where there has been copyright infringement in adaptation work. In one case[61], the defendant Artic International had intensified its computer work to accelerate the action of the plaintiff's video game. The court,

---

[59]   Columbia Pictures, Ind. v. Aveco. Inc, 800 F.2d 59 3rd. Cir.1986
[60]   Indian Copyright Act, 1957Sec.2(a)
[61]   Midway Mfg.co v. Artic International, 704 F2d 965

however ruled that the defendant had adapted the work of the plaintiff and that there was a copyright infringement.

However, in another case[62], the court held that there was no work developed by the defendants and a enhancement of the original work to produce better results did not give rise to copyright violation.

Hence it depends upon the facts and circumstances of the case whether the defendant has adapted the work of the plaintiff. The comparison and the careful analysis of the two work form an essential part in determining the adaptation of the work.

Right to Prepare Derivative Works

Derivative work is based upon one or more pre existing Works in which a work may be recast, transformed or adopted and as a whole it represent the original works of authorship[63].

The federal court has held that a "Game Genie" device that altered features in Nintendo's videogame cartridges did not create a derivative work. The "Game Genie" enhanced the audiovisual display without incorporating the underlying work in any permanent from[64].

Web designers often examine various websites and select their most attractive features. The designers must be careful not to infringe on the copyright of author by preparing derivative work based on the original presentation. In each case, whether

---

[62]   Lewis galoob Toys v. Nintendo, 964 F2d965.

[63]   U.S.Copyright Act, 1976, sec 101

[64]   Lewis Galoob Toys, Inc. v. Nintendo, Inc, 964 F.2d 965

it amounts to copyright infringement or not, depends to a large extent upon the facts and circumstances of that particular case.

Digital technology and the Internet have challenged the very core of copyright Law. Copyright Law had its beginnings centuries ago, in a time were reproduction was difficult, yet it has survived into the twenty - first century where reproduction can be easier. Its resilience may well lie in its status as an economic right and the need to protect and reward intellectual creativity through economic channel.

Digital technology revolutionized the production, distribution and access to copyright work. New work in the form of multimedia has converged the existing media into one. It has improved the quality of the reproduction and transmission. It is also possible to have faster access to information that too through the Internet. This has challenged both the individual and public interests that copyright Law seek to protect. The rights of the authors, particularity reproduction and communication to the public through digital media are under serious threat. The traditional interpretation of the rights in the context of the existing technology is inadequate to product the interests of the authors and owners in Internet.

CHAPTER **III**

Basic Internet Challenges Regarding Author's Rights

"what is worth copying is prima-facie worth protecting[65]". This proposition through laid down about 100 years ago, is truer today.

Internet provides for the storage and distribution of literary, artistic audio and audio visual material held in digital format. Thus the digital nature of cyber technology makes digital copies being downloaded, copied and instantly distributed all over the world. Moreover the digital technology can provide perfect copies without any deterioration in quality[66]. Gross violations occur in cyber space due to the misconception that everything on the web is in public domain and therefore its use would not violate or infringe copyright. This view is further strengthened by another misconception that the law

---

[65] University of London press v. University of Tutorial Press. 1916(2)Ch601
[66] Rodney D.Ryder, Intellectual Property and Internet, Butterworths 2000. p425

only protects those material that display the proper copyright notice upon publication[67].But the nature of protection is that, works made by unknown author whose identity cannot be treated by reasonable enquiry is also protected by copyright[68].

Forms of Copyright Challenges in Internet

Like the traditional copyright infringement, if copyright materials are uploaded or downloaded without the permission of the copyright owner or author, it can lead to infringement of author's right in Internet. Accordingly, when representing an author, there is an interest in understanding, what Internet relatives will be regarded as potentially implicating the infringement of copyrighted works. Some of them are:-

1. Caching and mirroring
2. Linking
3. Framing
4. Pop-up advertising
5. Pee- to - peer systems
6. Archiving
7. Digital Audio Transmissions
8. Browsing etc..

---

[67] Rahul Matthan, Law relating to Computers and the internet, New Delhi, 2000 p.300

[68] Harry Cohen and Kenchia, E-Rights in Sterphen York and Kenchia, Ed. E-Commerce; A Guide to Law of electronic Business, London, Butterworths, 1999, p.142

Caching and mirroring

Caching is an activity in which a copy of material from an original source is stored for later use. So it is an automatic creation of temporary copies of digital data in order to make the data more readily available for subsequent use[69]. Whereas mirroring is the storing of the content of the entire website not only for reducing congestion but also for backing-up information stored in one server[70]. Both these system will badly affect the author's interest.

There are mainly two types of caching. Namely, local caching or client caching and proxy caching or server caching. In case of local caching the copies of material from the original source are available at the user level where as in case of proxy caching it is at the server level. Thus in the local caching the browser generally stores recently visited web pages in the RAM or on the hard disk of the end user's computer while in proxy caching, a copy of materials requested by users gets stored on a server other than the user's server. Generally the ISP stores' on its own servers, web pages that have been requested by its user's which attracts contributory or vicarious liability.

Although caching Is a sine qua non to the survival and continuing growth of Internet, for the benefit of intermediaries, content providers and users alike, it has potential of negatively affecting the interest of authors and right holders in documents

---

[69] David L. Hayes, The coming tidal wave of copyright issue on the internet (part III), Journal of Internal Law, August 1997, p.18

[70] Rodney D. Ryder, Intellectual Property and the Internet, Butterworths, 2000, p.429.

cached. Thus caching and mirroring are common techniques that were developed to enhance the liability of online content.

Caching a file usually affects the reproduction rights of the copyright owners[71]. In the case of mirroring also the compilation copyright of the server operator is affected through the reproduction of the entire group of mirrored files, It is to the extent of the selection or arrangement of file on the mirrored server which, is organized in a way that the reflects originality, as opposed to mechanical copying. Depending upon how the cached and mirrored works are delivered to the service provider's users, the reproduction, public display rights also may be affected.

Under E- commerce Directive[72], access providers are exempt from liabilities which might otherwise arise over automatic, intermediate and temporary storage of information solely for this purpose. This is subject to "Notice and Take -down conditions of the kind which also apply to Host ISPs[73]. Since there is also a danger that cached material will not contain the latest version of the original site. There are also obligations to comply with industry practice on updating content and technology for obtaining data on the use of the information[74].

Moreover the ECD[75]also provides for an explicit and automatic exemption for copies that are made incidental to use of work through a technological process such as transmission through a network or loading in to a memory for viewing or

---

[71]   ECD, 2001, Art.2.

[72]   Electronic Commerce Directive, 2001, Art. 13.

[73]   Ibid, Art.14.

[74]   Electronic Commerce Regulations, 2002, reg.18

[75]   ECD 2001, Art.5(1)

playing the work. The ECD has provided an optional exception to the reproduction right and the right of communication to the public[76].

In United States, the Congress has adopted a safe harbor provision under DMCA, it is an approach, limiting the potential liability for copyright infringement of service providers[77]. In order to take advantage of this limitation on liability, the service provider must not be the originator of the infringement material, must not modify the material, must update the cache regularly, must pass on to the copyright owner any user information that collected[78] and must be careful not be permit unauthorized access to materials that is restricted to the copyright owners subscription or to those who have issued a password by the copyright owner[79]. Although some caching will fall outside the scope of DMCA's Limitation on liability, some of the more traditional defenses to copyright infringement still may be applicable[80].

In a striking case[81], the court held that temporary copying while browsing is a functional equivalent of reading and hence does not enter the scope of copyright Laws. The process of temporary copying of the works on to RAM is somewhat similar to the act of a person going to a book shop and just

---

[76]   Ibid, Art.5(3)

[77]   ECD 2001, Art.5(3)

[78]   Such as the number of users who access the cached site.

[79]   OCILLA, 1998, Sec. 512 (b) (1)-(2).

[80]   The defenses may be fair use, implied license and consent by the owner of copyright in the cached material

[81]   Religious Technology Center v. Netcom Online Communication Service, 907 F.Supp. 1361, N.D.california, 1995.

looking at a book[82]. But the decision given in a previous case[83] was liable to be criticized and was not followed in many subsequent cases.

Practically speaking, one must appreciate that temporary copying on the RAM does not amount to copying violation and should be treated as a technical necessity. It may also not be wrong to say that the author who knows that such copying is obvious and incidental has impliedly given the authority for such copying[84]. The court therefore reiterated in a case[85], that the service provider does not directly infringe the reproduction, distribution or display rights when it is caching or mirroring as a result of automatic process. Such a result seems wise for several reasons, both in the context of Usenet news groups and in the context of automatic caching of website by a service provider[86].

As far as the liability of the ISP is concerned in India, the Information Technology Act clearly states that an ISP shall not be liable for any third -party information and data made available by him, if he proves that the offence was committed without his knowledge or that he had exercised due diligence to prevent the commission of such offence[87]. Although the act does not specifically deal with the concept of caching per se,

---

[82] Advanced Computer Services v. MAI System 845 F.Supp. 356 (E.D. va1994).

[83] MAI System Corp. v. Peak Computer Inc. 1991 F.2d51(8th Circuit, 1993)

[84] Pankaj Jain and Pandey Sangeet Rai, Copyright and Trademark laws Relating to Computers, Eastern book Co., 2005, p.57.

[85] Religious Technology Center v. Netcom Online Communication Services 907. F.Supp. 1361; N.D.California 1995.

[86] Playboy enterprises Inc. v.Frena 839.F.supp at 1552.

[87] Indian Information Technology Act, 2000, sec.79.

but the same can be read into Act, which provides stringent punishments for committing cyber crimes[88]. Thus any person who without the permission of the owner or any other person in charge accesses, downloads, copies or extracts any data from a computer system or network, including information or data held or stored in any removable storage medium shall be held liable for huge penalty[89]. Since IPS s cache the data without express permission of the owner of the web pages, it would be possible to punish the person who indulges in such act.

The implied license argument with respect to caching is a subject of discussion in the digital environment. The implied license theory would fall and counterproductive, if the right owners subjected such acts of caching. Moreover the theory implies that a license, if not implied, would be actually required[90]. The implied license argument will eventually fall apart of content owners are to succeed in claiming that, proxy caching requires their authorization as a matter of principles[91]. Failure to set a time to live on the part of website owner might well be interpreted as an implied license cache, by considering that it is a common knowledge among website owners and generally complied with by access providers[92].

---

[88] Ibid, sec. 43(b).

[89] Ibid, in which copying is mentioned as an offence

[90] David Nimmer, Brains and other Paraphernalia of the Digital Age, Harvard Journal of Law and Technology, 1996.p.20

[91] WCT, 1996 Art.7

[92] Bradford L. Smith, The Digital Agenda and Copyright; A content Providers Perspective, Paper presented at the sixth Annual Fordham International Conference New York, 1998 p.6.

Ephemeral Recording

Temporary copying is an issue which causes so much confusion and controversy in the digital context. In the early days of broadcasting and the so called ephemeral recording of protected works for the purpose of broadcasting and subsequent temporary archiving was an equally contested issue[93]. Then it was a matter for legislation in the countries to determine the regulations for ephemeral recording made by a broadcasting organization by means of its own facilities and use for its own broadcast[94]. Accordingly many nations adopted statutory licenses or limitations permitting the well established practice of ephemeral recording in the context of broad casting. ECD also support similar situation[95]. In contrast to the ECD[96], ephemeral recordings need not be transient or incidental, nor does the economic significance criterion apply.

Linking

Linking is an easy, user friendly and dynamic way of connecting documents[97]. It can be considered as the best known application of the Internet and World Wide Web[98].

---

[93] S. Bergerstorm, Radio Diffusion and its problems-An International Perspective, RIDA, 1959 p.323

[94] Berne Convention, 1971, Art.11(3)

[95] ECD, 2001, Art. 5(2)(d).

[96] Ibid, Art. 5(1)

[97] K. Beal the potential Liability of Linking on the internet; An Examination Of Possible Legal Solutions, Brigham Young University Law Review, 1998, p.704

[98] M. O. Rourke, Fencing Cyberspace; drawing boards in a virtual word, Minnesotta Law Review, 1998, p.631.

Linking permits a user to be automatically transported to a different page or a different website by clicking on an icon or on underlined text that appears on a web page. These icons or texts are referred to as hyperlinks or simply links. The ability to link to other sites makes the Internet such a valuable tool for locating information[99]. These so called links held's researchers to reach documents in complex networks more easily and efficiently[100]. As a powerful tool in the net, it has been very successful among users[101]. Thus, linking made the Internet, a channel for free distribution of information.

However, the process of linking has attracted many legal issues. Some site owners have demanded that before putting the link on their home page, linking site owners must seek permission from the site which is to be linked and failure to do so may violate their intellectual property rights. But hyper linking does not itself constitute direct copyright infringement by the operator of the linking site. When a hyperlink is executed, the user's web browser ceases communicating with the linking site and initiates a request to the linked site for transmission of the linked page. Thus, the linking site transmits none of the content of the linked page or the linked site to the user. The linking site also does not store any of the content of the likened site. It simply uses the Internet address of the site. Under these circumstances, none of the exclusive

---

[99]   Lisa T. Oratz and Matt Wagner, Copyright and the Internet. Technology business group, May 2001.

[100] Shea v. Reno, 930 F. supp 916,

[101] K. Stuckey, International Online Law journals Seminars Press Edition, 1998, p.657.

rights of the owner of the copyright in the linked site should be infringed by the linking site[102].

In case of surface linking, linking site owner cannot be held liable for copyright infringement because he is providing a link to the home page of the linked site and not to the inner pages. Moreover, it is the author of the linked site and not the linking site who reproduces the work for users. Surface links are simply addresses designating the location of a document on the web. They can be treated as references provided in footnotes. It is unlikely for courts to hold linking site owners liable for copyright infringement in surface linking for the reason that such a person has an implied license to provide link to every other page on the web. Further owner of linked sites generally know that the home page of their site can be referred to on the Internet for reference by other sites[103]. The Internet has been treated as an information superhighway and this providing a link to the home page of the linked site would not constitute copyright violation. Thus in surface linking, the linking site only provides an alternative method for viewing the linked the site.

In a Ninth Circuit court decision[104], when a user activates a link, RAM copies created on his computer. It could be argued that RAM copies created in computer are copies within the meaning of Copyright Act[105]. Other cases[106] have followed

---

[102] Ticket master Corp.v.Tickets.com Inc. 2003 WL 21406289

[103] Pankaj Jain and Pandey Sangeet Rai, Copyright and Trademark laws relating to Computers, Eastern book Co. 2005. p.152

[104] Sony Corp. of America v. Universal City Studios Inc., 464, U.S. 1984

[105] MAI System Corp. v. Peak Computers Inc., 991, F. 2d, 511, 9th Circuit, 1993.

[106] U.S. Copyright Act, 1976, Sec 102 (a)

the Ninth Circuit rulings, and implies that, linking involves copying.

In case of deep linking, it is not clear that an implied license could apply when the link is made to one of the site's interior pages, thus circumventing the main page and the advertising placed on it. Deep linking issue were highlighted in U.S. Courts in the year 1997[107]. In an interesting case[108], Ticketmaster sued the Tickets. Com for deep linking, in which it was held that hyper linking itself did not involve copying because the customer is transferred by the link to the genuine site. But in another case the court adopted an opposite view[109]. To avoid copyright infringement of third party by deep linking, the simplest thing is to obtain consent before deep linking to any third party site. One should also avoid using copyright works as hyperlinks. Website owners that wish to protect themselves against deep linking should ensure that, times and conditions include prohibition against deep linking and aggregating and these terms and conditions are accepted by Internet users before access to the site, is granted as cost permitting and it may also be a worth investing in technical methods for the prevention of deep linking[110].

Deep linking attracts contributory infringement in many cases. A claim against a party who aid in another's infringement

---

[107] Marobie FL Inc v. National Association of Fire & Equipments Distributers, 983 F.Supp. 1167. N.D. 111, 1997

[108] Ticket master v. Microsoft, U.S. Code. No. 97-3055, DP, 1997

[109] Ticketmaster v.Tickets.com Inc., 54 U.S.P.Q 2d 1344-1345.C.D. California 2000.

[110] E-bay Inc. v. Bidders Edge Inc., No-992/200, RMW. N.D.California, 2000.

is permitted under U.S[111] and U.K[112].Law. That is interpreted as infringement[113].

In a remarkable case[114], the plaintiffs sought an injunction against the defendant's web site that contained the URLs of three web sites that the defendant knew contained infringing copies of the plaintiff's Church Handbook of Instructions. The court concluded that when a user browses a website, a copy is made to permit viewing of the material and that in making a copy, even a temporary one, such person infringes the copyright, when permission is absent from the copyright owner[115]. The court in contributing infringement[116], in addition to providing the URL of the site with the infringing material, the defendants clearly knew the material on the third party infringing and actively encouraged people to go to these web site and download the handbook.

But the above mentioned case does not mean that all sites that link to infringing site are liable for contributory infringing[117]. The court found direct or contributing infringement in case, where the site linked to a site that linked to several other site, one of which contained infringing material[118].

---

[111]   Michel Chissick, Electronic Commerce; Law and practice, Third Ed., Sweet and Maxwell, 2202, p.150-151.

[112]   U.S. Copyright Act, 1976, sec.106

[113]   CDPA, 1988, Sec.16(2)

[114]   CBS Songs v. Amsrad, 1988 A.C. 1058

[115]   Intellectual Reserve, Inc. v. Utah Light House Ministry Inc., 75 F.Supp. 2d 1290

[116]   Ibid

[117]   bid, 1295

[118]   Bernstein v. JC Penney Inc.1998 U.S. Dist. Lexis 19048 C.D. California.

In another case[119], one newspaper linked to specific items in another, by giving the precise headlines used by the other on its website. In Interim proceedings, this activity was found likely to constitute copyright infringement. But the general requirements of infringement has to be applied and linking can certainly be organized without any such borrowing of expression[120]. An objection under U.K. Law could be sustained only if there were an infringement of a database right or if consumers were being misled about source so as to constitute passing off. In countries with a broader conception of unfair competition liability, there may be greater scope for legal intervention[121].

In case of linking and its normative objective, court must evaluate whether enjoining a like as distinguished from the infringing content at the linked to site is necessary to preserve copyright incentive. Otherwise there is only little justification for liability[122].

The DMCA and Electronic Commerce Directive and European Copyright Directive has provided certain safe harbors for service providers. These provisions suggest that linking will not be freely permitted on the web. The exception of liability means that if a service provider sets a link does not comply with one or more of the condition, it will be liable. This seems to accept the theory that RAM copies are copies in the meaning of the Copyright Act, because the like provider

---

[119]   Ibid
[120]   Shetland Times v. Wills (1997) F.S.R.604
[121]   Ticket master v. Ticket.com (2000)Lexis 12987
[122]   Stepstone v. U.K. officer, Financial Times January 18, 2001 (Germany)

could never be contributorily liable[123]. However, the service providers are going to held liable when linked website is very clearly violating the rights of the copyright owner, because actual knowledge is required[124]. The position in a case[125] is that even where the operators of the linking site assumed that the linked sites facilitated the downloading of unauthorized copies, however, such circumstantial evidence of the linking sites involvement in the infringing activity may be inadequate at the summary judgment stage.

More over the doctrine of fair use can be a defense for linking site owners only if such site owners fulfils the factors laid down in copyright law[126]. However, when the use is commercial and is primarily for the purpose of encroaching the interest of the owner then the linking site owner can directly be held liable when copyrighted work, is placed as a link[127]. Even though linking attracts many copyrightable issues, as the court concluded in a case[128], linking is analogous to using a library's card index to find reference to particular items.

---

[123]   Richard Gilburt and Michael A. Katz, When good Value Chains Go bad; Remarks on The economics of Indirect Liability And Contributory Infringement of Copyright, Hastings Law Journal, 2001, p. 343..

[124]   R. Morris, be careful to whom you link; How Internet Practices of hyper linking and Framing Pose new challenges to Establish trade mark and Copyright Law, Rutgers Law journal, 1998, p.287

[125]   D. Alweiss, Copyright Infringement on the Internet; can the Wild West Be tamed? Touro Law Review, 1999 p.1942.

[126]   Arrista Records Inc.v.Mp3 Board Inc, 2002, U.S.Dist LEXIS 16165m 10-14(S.D.N.Y. Aug 29, 2002)

[127]   U.S. Copyright Act, 1976, Sec.107.

[128]   Leslie A. Kelly v. Arriba Soft Corp. 280 F 3d 934 (9th Circuit, 2002).

Framing

Framing is another important issue on the world wide web that has become a source of controversy[129]. Framing refers to an HTML code which allows web page creators to divide the browser window into separate sub windows; usually called frames[130]. The content of each frame is taken from different web pages, allowing the display of more than one webpage at once. Usually, this technique is used to display one static frame with ownership information, advertisements and a table of contents and one dynamic frame containing the actual information of interest to the user, which will exclusively be updated if new information is retrieved[131]. In this way, site owner can incorporate websites, in part or as a whole, produced third parties and surround and juxtapose them with their own logos, advertisement and materials. While the URL address shown remains that of their own framing site[132].

Due to the technical process of framing, since no part of the website is reproduced by the linking site and the reproduction right of the owner is not clearly involved with respect to the provider of the link. However, the user creates a RAM copy that can arguably be a derivative work under U.S. Law[133]. Then the question becomes whether a derivative work

---

[129] Ticket master v. Tickets.com, 2000, LEXIS, 12987.

[130] Meeka Jun, Being Framed? Imposters beware; New York Law journal. jun 20.1997.

[131] Rodney D.Ryder, Intellectual Property and the Internet, Butterworths, 2000, p.429.

[132] Ibid

[133] The URL remains that of the Framing Site Even if the user follows a link from any pages within the frame.

has been created. If a derivative work is created, the user can be direct infringer and the like provider is contributorily liable.

According to a Ninth Circuit court decision[134], the defendant was liable when he resold some pictures he had previously purchased, mounted on tiles, and in a 7th circuit court decision[135] it was held that buying notes cards and mounting them on ceramic tiles do not create a derivative work in the sense f Copyright Act. Another important case[136] that should be taken into this fields is that, the audio visual displays produced by a device called Game Genie, which altered Nintendo games as they appeared on the screen, did not constitute derivative works. The same position was adopted in another case[137].

In case of framing, the existence of an implied license to frame is difficult to sustain because framing is a relatively new development, and the website owners did not necessarily take into account when they posted their materials on the web. Moreover the court have noted that a license to make a derivative work is only granted if the copyright owner entitled to do so[138]. The fair use defence also doubtfully applies in framing. In U.S. this issue came into attention in 1997[139].

---

[134]   U.S. Copyright Act, 1976, sec.106(2)

[135]   Mirage Editions Inc. v. Albuquerque, A.R.T.Co.856 F.2d.1341, 9th Circuit, 1988.

[136]   Lee v.A.R.T.Co.964 F.2d965.7th Circuit, 1992.

[137]   Lewis Galoob Toys inc. v. Nintendo Inc., 964 F 2d.965 9th circuit, 1995.

[138]   Microstar v. Forgmen, 154, F.3d.1107, 9th circuit, 1998.

[139]   J. B. ko, Parasites, The case for hyper linking as a copy right infringement, Loyola L. A. Entertainment Law journal, 1998, p.361.

The position in a case is that framing can be actionable under copyright Law[140]. From the legal practioners standpoint, the use of framing technology combined with hyperlinks raises several significant issues that have been subject of litigation[141]. In a striking case, plaintiff news publishers alleged that, the defendant's website used a frame structure and hyperlinks to the plaintiff's own websites to alter user's perusal of the plaintiff's sites in a variety of ways, including the imposition of the defendant's boarder containing the paid advertising of the defendant's advertisers[142]. The complaint alleged copyright infringement, commercial misappropriation of the plaintiff's content under the "hot news" doctrine, trademark dilution and infringement and tortuous interference with the plaintiff's own advertising contracts, among other action. The action was settled before the merits were reached. The court ordered settlement, provided that the defendants would cease framing the plaintiff's web site and that the defendant's would link to the plaintiff's sites only with permission[143], with such permission revocable upon fifteen days notice by the plaintiffs[144].

---

[140] Washington post Company v. Total news Inc., 97 civ.1990. SDNY, February 20, 1997.

[141] Journal Gazette Co. v.mid west Internet exchange, 98 W 0130, N.D.indiana.

[142] M. Luria, Controlling Web Advertising: Spanning, Linking, Framing and privacy, Computer Lawyer, 1997, p.13

[143] Washington Post Co. v. Total news Inc., 97 civ. 1990, SDNY, February 20, 1997.

[144] That is a 'link license'

In another case[145], AAI, the owner of the registered service mark I-800-DENTIST, granted an exclusive licence to Futuredontics to use the mark in connection with its dental referral business. Futuredontics established a corporate website, which it registered with the copyright office. Without seeking, Futuredontic's permission, AAI subsequently linked its own website to certain Futuredontics web pages, which were surrounded by a frame featuring the AAI logo, information on AAI, and "links to all of AAI's other web pages[146]". Futuredontics used AAI, claiming both copyright and trademark infringement. AAI moved to dismiss the copyright infringement claim, arguing that the framed version of the Futuredontics web page did not constitute an unauthorized derivative work and the Futuredontics had not stated an infringement claim. The District court disagreed, ruling that AAI had been able to show as a matter of law that the framed Futuredontics web page did not qualify as a derivation work.

There are a variety of ways in which framing could constitute infringement of a linked site's copyright. The reproduction right may be infringed in that, when the linked site is locally cached, the reproduction occurs for the purpose of framing rather than displaying, without the copyright owner's permission. The infringed adaptation right may be infringed if the framed work is deemed to be an unauthorized derivative work of the linked site[147]. Finally, the public display

---

[145] Jenny Lyn Balder, old media, Meet New Media: Forget those old –fashioned Footnotes, Hyperlink, New York Times, July 16, 2000

[146] Futuredonitics. Inc v. Applied Angramatics, Inc., 45 U.S.P.Q 2d 2005

[147] Ibid

and performance rights may be infringed on the grounds that the linking site is altering the linked site operator's intended manner of displaying or performing the content on its site[148].

In a remarkable case, two professional sports leagues and several major entertainment companies used Canadian website that rebroadcast, without permission, television programming, including plaintiffs copyrighted programs, in a frame surrounded by advertising, arranged by the site. The court enjoined the web site's operations; finding, that the rebroadcast framed or not, infringed plaintiff's right of public performance[149].

In Germany, the extraction and utilization of extracts from a medical dictionary in an electronic from was held to constitute infringement both of the copyright in the data base and the sui generis database right when the material was placed within the defendant's own frame[150].

Pop-Up Advertising

The related issue of farming is that of pop- up advertisement. It has raised a number of law suits[151]. Typically, plaintiffs, who are website operators that object to pop-up advertisements interfering with the presentation of their sites, have raised both copyright and trademark infringement claims. On the copyright front, plaintiffs have alleged

---

[148]   Mirage editions Inc v. Alburqurque, A.R.T.Co.56 F.2d 1341, 9th circuit

[149]   Ticket Master Corp. v. Tickets.com Inc 200 WL 21406289

[150]   National Football League v. TV Radio Corp. 53 U.S.P.Q 2d 2000

[151]   Medizinches Lexicon I, Hamburg

violation of both display right[152] and derivative works right[153]. Thus so far, courts have uniformly rejected claims based on copyright infringement. In rejecting the claim, that pop-up advertisement violate the public display right of the copyright owner, website operator -plaintiffs, courts have noted that the software that delivers pop-up advertisements does not show or display plaintiff's copyrighted works. One court noted that pop-up advertisements do not actually appear on websites. The apparent overlay is the result of a distinct transmission of data to the user's computer[154]. It them considered plaintiff's contention that because the display of pop- up advertisements alters the video memory of a computer, the advertisements infringe the plaintiff's copyright[155].

When a pop-up advertisement appears on the screen, it alters the content of the video memory, the altering the plaintiff's copyrighted webpage and displaying a modified version of the webpage. The court rejected this line of reasoning, noting first that the video memory simply contains a pixel- by snapshot of whatever happens to be displayed on a computer screen at any given instant[156]. Given that these pixels are part of the user's physical computer and plaintiff copyright holders could claim no ownership over them[157]. The video memory changes when there is any modification of the

---

[152] In re Gator Corp. Software and copyright Litigation, 259 F.Supp. 2d 1378 (J.P.M.L. 2003) (Nine actions against Gator.com and three against u.com etc)

[153] U.S Copyright Act, 1976, Sec.106(5)

[154] Ibid, 106 (2)

[155] Well Fargo and Co. case, 293 F.Supp. 2d at 747

[156] Plaintiff argued that, the video memory contains a copy or snapshot of their copyrighted webpage.

[157] Wells Fargo and Co. Case 293 F.Supp. 2d 747

on -screen display[158]. The court suggest that, the plaintiff's theory would make an infringer out of every user who clicked an icon or scrolled through a document that happened to be open at the same time they were viewing the plaintiff's websites. The court then concluded that, "accordingly the alteration of video memory does not constitute a modification of the plaintiff's web pages".

Moreover, pop-up advertisements does not constitute unauthorized derivate works of plaintiff's website[159]. One court held that the brief nature of the contents of a users video memory cannot satisfy a requirement that a derivative work be fixed in order to be infringing[160]. The pixels on a computer screen are updated every $1/70^{th}$ of a second. The alteration is therefore far too transitory an occurrence to from a basis for copyright violation[161].

Peer- to-Peer systems

Peer to peer system also brings cases, where additional services are part of an Internet Information package[162]. The MP3 player for recorded music allows CD or other digital recording to be compressed to a degree which enables rapid transfer of its contents without significant loose of quality. Likewise with DVD for films. There, the core issue is the

---

[158] Ibid

[159] That is when the users drag the cursor across the screen with the mouse

[160] Ibid

[161] Ibid. The court granted an injunction on the ground that pop-up advertisements were likely to confuse consumers.

[162] Massey (2001) Ent. L.R.128

misuse of the peer to peer technology (P2P)[163]. Through this technology even though the exchange of data occurs directly between the two computers, the initial linking is done with the help of ISPs. This case bringing up the crucial question of responsibility of the service providers.[164]

Napster website provided free software for peer -to - peer connections between its users, facilitating the upload and download and of MP3 files by its users. In California, Napster's service was held to constitute both vicarious and contributory infringement of copyright works, which were being provided free but without license from the copyright owner[165]. It is pertinent to note that Napster provided technical support for the indexing and searching of MP3 files.[166]

The free software provided by Napster Music share enabled the users to (1) make MP3 music files stored on individual computer hard drives available for copying by other Napster users(2) search for MP3 music files stored on other user's computers and (3) transfer exact copies of the contents of other user's MP3 files from one computer to another via Internet[167]. There was further evidence of Napster's active involvement with users, as it provided technical support for the indexing and searching of MP3 files, as well as for its other functions, including a chat room, where users could meet to discuss

[163] RIAA v. Napster Inc. 114, F.Supp. 2d.896, N.D.California, 2000
[164] R. Mohanakrishna, The Law v. Technology; Napster Case, The Hindu, 17 November 2000
[165] A&M records V Napster Inc, 239 F. Supp 3d 1004
[166] Akester P, Copyright and the P2P Challenge, European Intellectual Property Review, 27 (3) (2005) 106 -112
[167] A & M Records v. Napster Inc, 239 F.3d, 1004 at 1011

music and a directory, where participating artists could provide information about their music[168]. On being used by copyright holders, Napster contended that it is exempted from liability because its software and network were capable of substantial non - infringing uses[169] based on Sony doctrine.[170] However, there after a starting fact that come out was that about 87 percent of the material available on Napster was copyrighted and that the plaintiffs held the copyrights of about 70 percent of this material, which clearly established the infringement prong.[171]

The court concluded that, Napster had constructive knowledge of infringement that was taking place and they had requisite means to stop infringement by denying access.[172] Moreover, Napster was facilitating and helping the user by maintaining indexing central servers and providing technical support to it users.[173] The court stated, without the support services defendant provides, Napster users could not find and download the music files they want, with the ease of which

---

[168] Ibid

[169] Anderws TK, Control content, not innovation; Why Hollywood should embrace peer-to-peer technology despite the MGM v. Grokster Battle, Loyola Los Angeles Entertainment Law review, 25 (2005) 92.

[170] Sony Corp. of America v. Universal City Studios Inc., 464 US (984) 417.

[171] Myrick RM, Peer-to-peer and substantial non-infringing use: Giving the term 'substantial' some meaning, Journal of Intellectual Property Law, 12 (2005) 546.

[172] A & M Records Inc. v. Napster, Inc.239 F. 3d 1004 at 1029.

[173] Moye JM, How Sony survived: Peer-to-peer software, Grokster, and contributory copyright Liability in the twenty-first-century, North Carolina Law Review, 84(2006) 663.

defendant boast[174] and liable for infringement and subsequently injunction was granted against P2P network.

Archiving

The digital era often concentrates on the accessibility of content because it consists of bits rather than atoms.[175] However, International regulations about copyright protection[176] are increasingly restrictive with respect to the availability of protected content. We are facing a contradictory period in which while it was possible to allow very body who comes to a library to borrow a book, without infringing any copyright rule, it may be forbidden to create a digital edition of the same content for the same library user.

If a single service provider is to make the majority available content accessibility, it will be a unique challenge, but whatever is omitted from that archive could be missing forever and for the vast majority of people. According to a survey,[177] it appears that many students use the web as their only source of information. They rely mainly on one search engine and rarely check the information they find from the first source they access. Here, though not raising the controversial issue of censorship, but even

---

[174] A & M Records, Inc. v. Napster Inc, 239 F. 3d 1004 at 1022.

[175] Negroponte, N., Being Digital, London: Hodder and Stoughton, 1995, p.36

[176] Numerico, T. and Bowen J.P., Copyright and Promotion: Oxymoron or Opportunity? In J. Hemsley v. Cappellinni and G. Stanke (eds)., EVA 2005 London Conference Proceedings, University College London, UK, 25-29 July.

[177] Graham, L. and Metaxas, P.T., Of Course it's true; I saw it on the Internet!, Communications of the ACM, Vol. 46, No.5 pp 71-75, 2003

without an explicit will to control information, a single source for all available literature seems like an undesirably and potentially dangerous situation. According to Derrida[178], we have to face the fact that an archive is both revolutionary and conservative and that those who control the archive exercise a violent effect on history and consequently on society in its entirety.

There are two reasons for searching online, to discover that which we know exists on the web, and to discover that which we assume must be there.[179] In practice, when considering the copyright of digital materials for archival purpose, is circumscribed by two problems, which can be considered as technical and legal fencing. The case with which digital materials can be copies and the fidelity of the copies means that those who create the materials or who have acquired property rights, in them, risk losing control over their reproduction. However, the degree of investment, skill and effort required to make illegal copy of a digital work is often significantly lower than that which was previously required to make a copy of a tangible work. Thus, right holders in digital materials have increasingly begun to seek to retain control over their dissemination by restricting the practice of copying, using technical means.

The DMCA and ECD provides protection through ant circumvention provision. Further, to provide counterbalance the DMCA provides certain exemptions to archival purpose.[180]

---

[178] Derrida, J. Archive Fever, Chicago: University of Chicago Press, 1996

[179] Band J. The Google Print Library Project: A copyright Analysis, Policy bandwidth.com, Washington DC, USA, August 2005, p.32

[180] DMCA, 1998, Sec.404.

The web was originally based on the freedom of all users to share interesting information and we need to pursue the same objective when inventing new tools for accessing it now and in the future to continue the original spirit of the web and the social power of collectively creating an online archive. Open initiatives such as Wikipedia, and to a lesser extent so far Wiki books, are allowing a certain amount of increased democratization of knowledge by individual in the cultural and other fields.[181]

Digital Audio Transmissions

To address the concerns of copyright owners in sound recordings, the Digital performance Right in sound Recordings Act of 1995 Act of 1995 added to the list of copyright owner's exclusive rights the right of public performance by digital audio transmission[182]. The Act, however, also added provisions, later further amended by the DMCA, exempting from infringement liability certain digital audio transmissions of sound recording and providing a statutory licensing scheme for other digital audio transmissions that were not specifically exempted. These provisions are intended to address recent technological developments that permit transmission of sound recording via the Internet. They are supplied with qualifications and limitations and should be carefully examined the issues relating to digital audio transmission of sound recordings.[183]

---

[181] Bowen, J.P. and Angus, J., Museums and Wikipedia. In D. Berman and J. Trant (eds) MW2006: 'Museums and the web 2006, Albuquerque, New Mexico, USA, March 2006.

[182] U.S Copyright Act, 1976, Sec. 106(6).

[183] Ibid, Sec. 114.

A public performance of sound recording by means of a digital audio transmission is exempt from infringement liability if the transmission is not offered as part of an "interactive service."[184] There are also provisions for statutory license.[185]The Librarian of congress established rates for the period 1998-2002, with the small Webcaster settlement Act providing an alternative approach for small and non-commercial web casters. Moreover there is provision regarding the distribution of royalties from the digital public performance of sound recordings.[186]

Browsing

"Browsing" encompass a variety of activities including viewing the contents of websites. In most cases, browsing not to be viewed as triggering the reproduction right unless a substantial portion of the work is copied for more than a transitory period.[187] The work must be fixed in order to trigger the reproduction rights, but whether temporary storage in computer RAM during the course of browsing session would qualify as fixation remains uncertain. Where, as is common, a copy of a web pages is cached locally on the user's hard drive for later retrieval and viewing, fixation has occurred.

Browsing also may trigger the public performance and public display rights of the copyright owner,[188] depending on the work browsed, the recipient's use of the work and whether

---

[184]   U.S Copyright Act, 1976, Sec. 114 (1)(7).

[185]   Ibid, Sec. 114 (f).

[186]   Ibid, Sec. 114 (g).

[187]   Ibid, Sec. 102 (a).

[188]   Ibid, Sec. 106.

the work is perceived simultaneously with its transmission or whether it is delayed. In addition, in the case of a sound recording, the public digital performance right may apply, if none of the exemptions to that right pertain. Similarly, as in the case of uploading, the display right may be triggered in the case of library, visual and other works that are, in fAct, displayed to the user during browsing process. The triggering of the display right, is depended upon whether the display can be deemed as display to the public."

Depending upon the specific facts surrounding these acts of browsing, even if the technically trigger one or more of the exclusive rights[189] of copyright, they still may not be infringing because such acts may constitute fair uses. Particularly when the reproduction, performance or display is made of only a fragment of a work, for transitory period,[190] for non-commercial use and when downloading occurs, the argument that browsing is a fair use would seem strong.

In this famous case,[191] the court discussed browsing at some length and concluded that browsing of textual work was probably protected by fair use or that, at most, such browsing constituted innocent infringement.[192] As the court rationally observed, the "temporary copying involved in browsing is only necessary because humans cannot otherwise perceive digital information. It is the functional equivalent of reading, which does not implicate the copyright laws and may be done by

---

[189] Owner has two kinds of rights, economic rights and moral rights.

[190] U.S Copyright Act, 1976, Sec. 102.

[191] Religious Technology Center v. Netcom Online Communication Services, 907 F.Supp. 1361.

[192] Ibid.

anyone in a library without the permission of the copyright owner."[193] In other words, denying users a limited right to browse online material would effectively make the Internet unusable, because that material cannot be located or viewed without arguably triggering at least some of the copyright owner's exclusive rights.

Activities Protected under DMCA safe Harbors and its Interpretation

Even if an online service provider's conduct is not within the scope of the fair use defense, it may be insulated from monetary liability under the "safe harbor" provision of the DMCA. Conversely, if the service provider does not fall within the DMCA's "safe harbors", it may still escape liability for direct infringement if its conduct is not volitional. DMCA provides expressly that the statutes are neither exclusive nor do they preempt the common law standards of direct and contributory liability.[194] The fourth circuit court has held that even if a service provider falls outside a DMCA safe harbor as its conduct still may not rise to the level of direct infringement. Accordingly, post DMCA, service providers may continue to invoke all available and applicable affirmative defenses and may otherwise argue that their conduct does not rise to the level of a prima facie case of infringement. In short, the

---

[193] Ibid.

[194] Costar Group Inclusive v. Loop net Inclusive, 2004 U.S. App. LEXIS 12123, 19-28.

DMCA's safe harbor for service providers is "a floor, not a ceiling, of protection.[195]

The DMCA recognizes many different roles played by online service providers and creates incentives for providers to co –operate with copyright owners in situations where the service providers have both specific knowledge of potential infringement and the ability to stop it. For most purposes, the DMCA defines a "service provider" as a provider of online services or network access, or operator of facilities therefore.[196]

Because ISP's merely act as conduits for information sharing, they also have an added protection from the DMCA's subpoena provisions, which compel ISPs to disclose the identities of alleged infringers.[197] The D.C Circuit has held that the section 512 (h) cannot issue against the ISPs because they have no ability to "remove" or "disable access to infringing material, a requirement of the DMCA's subpoena and notification provisions.[198]

For many legal practitioners, an important question is whether these safe harbors would be applicable to many typical website rather than traditional ISPs. The definition of "service provider" has been interpreted broadly by the courts.[199] A website permitting users to post and access commercial real

---

[195]   Religious Technology Center v. Netcom Online Communication services, 907 F.Supp. 1361, the court also rejected plaintiff's claims of direct infringement against the bulletin board operator, Klemesurd.

[196]   OCILLA 1998, Sec. 512 (k) (1) (B).

[197]   Ibid, Sec. 512 (h).

[198]   RIAA v. Verizon Internet Services, (Inre Verizon Internet Services), 351 F 3d 1229.

[199]   ALS scan v. Remer Q. Cmtys Inc. 239 F 3d 619.

estate listings, the online auction site e-Bay,[200] and an Internet services that verifies the age of visitors to participating adult website, all qualified as through them, "service providers" under the DMCA.[201] One court even extended the protection of the DMCA's safe harbors to e-Bay's employees on the rationale that the harbors would not be effective if plaintiffs could circumvent them by suing a service employees.[202]

In another case, the service, which routed communications between file sharers, was deemed to be a service provider, Indeed the District court stated that the definition so broad that it would "have trouble imagining existence of an online service that would not fall under the definition".[203] Nevertheless, as noted below, some websites for which public access is unrestrained and no subscription agreement is required, would not be entitled to invoke any safe harbors in connection with litigation involving infringing content on, or available. The DMCA expressly limits the potential direct liability of service providers in connection with four activities:-

- Acting as a conduit for infringing material
- Caching infringing material
- Strong infringing material at the direction of a user, and
- Providing access to infringing materials.[204]

---

[200] Hendrickson v. e Bay Inc. 165 FSupp. 2nd 1082.
[201] Perfect 10, Inc. v. Cybernet Ventures Inc., 213 F.Supp. 2d 1146 (CD California, 2002).
[202] Hendrickson v. e Bay, Inc. 165 FSupp. 2d 1082.
[203] Inre Aimster Copyright Litigation, 334 F.3d 643 (7th cir. 2003).
[204] OCILLA, 1998, sec. 512 (a)-(d).

For each one of these Limitation on liability, the DMCA provides detailed compliance requirements for online service providers. In all cases, however the service provider must have no actual knowledge of the infringement.

In addition, to qualify for protection under the DMCA, a service provider must agree to terminate subscribers who engage in repeated acts of infringement, must notify users of this policy, and must accommodate standard technological measures used by copyright owners to identify or protect their works, such as digital water marks: In other words, a service provider must have "subscribers", which implies some sort of contractual arrangement.

Court are split regarding the extent to which a service provider must actively terminate repeat infringers and\ or actively monitor for infringement to qualify for the safe harbors. The District court in a case rejected the defendant's "persistent attempts to invoke the protection of section 512", because it found that the defendants were "aware of facts or circumstances from which infringing activity is apparent" and did not act to remove or disable access to the infringing materials.[205] The Ninth Circuit court also found that there were significant questions regarding Napster's status as a service provider and adequacy of Napster's compliance policy.[206] Other courts have differed as to whether a service provider must actually implement a policy and terminate repeat infringers,[207] or merely impress upon their subscribers a

---

[205] A & M Records Inc. v. Napster Inc., 54 US PQ 2d (BNA) 1746(N.D.Cal.2002) (holding that the Napster Online service does not qualify for the section 512 safe harbor).

[206] Ibid.

[207] Ibid.

"realistic threat" of termination for repeated infringement.[208] Presumably, the obligation to "terminate" does not require extra ordinary technological measures to guarantee that the terminated subscriber cannot re subscribe under a new account or cannot use another account.[209] In one case[210] involving America Online, the Ninth Circuit court concluded that ISP had not "reasonably implemented its policy against repeat infringers" because it closed the e-mail address for infringement notifications and failed to provide for forwarding of message from the old account. When the service provider functions as a pure conduit of information, the DMCA bars any monetary damages and permits only certain type of injunctions. To benefit from this limitation, however, a service provider must meet certain requirements.

The provider must be an entity that transmits, routes, or provides connections for the infringing content and the infringing transmission cannot be initiated by the provider. Further the infringing transmission must be routed or stored temporarily through an "automatic technical process" without modifying its content and the provider cannot select the recipients of the infringing material, and it cannot place the infringing material, in a manner "ordinarily accessible" to those other than the designated recipients.[211]

This safe harbors does not require service to remove or block access to infringing materials on receiving notification of infringement…….[212] A service provider that caches infringing

---

[208]   Ellison v. Robertson, 189, F.Supp. 2d 1051.
[209]   Ibid.
[210]   Ibid.
[211]   OCILLA, 1998, Sec. 512 (a).
[212]   Ellison v. Robertson, 189 F Supp 2d 1051.

material may be able to rely on another part of the DMCA[213] that bars any monetary liability and permits only certain types of injunctions with respect to caching.[214]

Effective notification of a claimed infringement must be made in writing to the service provider's designated agent and must include substantially; (a) a physical or electronic signature of a person authorized to act for the owner of an exclusive right allegedly infringed (b) identification of the allegedly infringed copyrighted work or a representative list in the case of multiple copyrighted works at a single online site.(c) Identification of the allegedly infringing material and information reasonably sufficient to permit the service provider to locate and remove the material,(d) information reasonably sufficient to permit the service provider to contact the complaining party, such as address, phone number, and, if available, e-mail address,(e) a statement that the complaining party has a good faith belief that the use of the materials is not authorized by the copyright owner, its agent or the law, and (f) a statement that the information in the notice is accurate, and, on penalty of perjury, that the complaining party is authorized to act for owner of an axclucive right allegedly infringed.[215] In one case[216] MPAA's take -down notice to Internet service provider satisfied good faith belief requirement where website contained statement suggesting users could download full length moves from site. This subsection also contains

---

[213] OCILLA 1998, Sec. 512 (c) (3)(A).
[214] Ibid, Sec 512 (b).
[215] Ibid, Sec. (c) (3) (A).
[216] Rossi v. Motion Picture Association of America, U.S.P.Q. 2d, 1047.

detailed provisions for determining whether notification is in substantial compliance.[217]

In another case[218] plaintiff owner of copyrights in erotic images substantially complied with the DMCA's notification requirements when it, identified two sites created for the sole purpose of infringing plaintiff's copyrights asserted that virtually all images on the two sites were its copyrighted materials and referred defendant to two web addresses where it could find pictures of plaintiff's models and obtain plaintiff's copyright information.

In a case[219] defendant not entitled to safe harbor where it imposed requirements on copyright owners beyond those in the DMCA. But in another case[220] plaintiff did not comply substantially with notice requirement by informing online action service in writing that counterfeit copies of a video were being sold because he failed to identify them by e Bay item numbers and not all copies with title mentioned in letter were alleged to be unauthorized.

In case of caching,[221] the service provider must update the cache regularly, must pass to the originator any user information collected and must be careful not to permit unauthorized access to material that is restricted to the orignator's subscribers or those who have been issued a password by the originator. In addition, the service provider, must not be the original source

---

[217] OCILLA, 1998, Sec. (c) (3) (B).
[218] ALS scan inc. v. Remar Q Cmtys Inc., 239, F.3d 619, 625.
[219] Perfect 10 Inc. v. Cybernet Venture Inc. 167 FSupp. 2d 1114.
[220] Hendrickson v. e-Bay Inc., 165 F supp 2d 1082.
[221] OCILLA, 1998, Sec.512(b).

of the infringing materials, must not modify this material through an automatic technical process.[222]

In connection with material uploaded by a third party to a service provider's server, such as postings to a BBS or a website, the service provider generally is not liable for money damages if it does not have actual knowledge of infringing material, "is not aware of facts or circumstances from which infringing activity is apparent"[223] and does not receive any financial benefit directly from the infringing activity in situations where the service provider has control over such activity.[224] Also when a service provider is presented with notice of a claimed infringement in the format directed by the DMCA, or when it obtains actual knowledge of an infringement, it must expeditiously[225] to remove the infringing material.[226]

In order for search engines and online directories with hyperlink to functions, property, another limitation on liability applies to service providers who provide references, pointer or hyperlink to sites that contain infringing material.[227] The requirement for taking advantage of this defence are similar to those mentioned in the preceding paragraphs with respect to

---

[222] Ibid

[223] This test is referred to in the legislative history as imposing a constructive "red flag" test, which seeks to prevent service providers from ignoring prevalent infringement by consciously avoiding acquiring actual knowledge, HOUSE COMMITTEE ONE THE JUDICIARY, 105TH CONG, 2 DSESS, SECTION-BY-SECTION ANALYSIS OF H.R. 2281 at 28.

[224] OCILLA, 1998, Sec. 512 (c) (1),(d).

[225] Costar Group Inc. v. Loopnet Inc., 2004 U.S. App. LEXIS 123, 19-28.

[226] OCILLA, 1998, Sec. 512 (c),(d).

[227] Ibid, Sec. 512 (c),(d).

material uploaded by users, including that the service provider may not benefit financially from any infringing activity over which it has control.[228]

In the Napster litigation, the District court concluded that Napster was ineligible for this safe harbor, because it could police its service by monitoring the indexing function, and even though Napster did not charge a fee, the court pointed to the defendants plan to make money through" one of several generation revenue models".[229] Finally in order to provide incentive providers to remove potentially infringing material, the DMCA, limits the liability of service provider for taking down such material so long as the party that uploaded the allegedly infringing material receives prompt notification I f its removal and is given the opportunity to request formally that the material be put pack.[230] A formal counter- notification requesting the restoration of removed material must include the physical or electronic signature of the requesting party, identification of the material that was removed, a sworn statement that the requesting of the material that was removed, a statement that the requesting party has a good faith belief that the material was taken down as a result of mistaken or misidentification, and the requesting party's name, address telephone number and consent to jurisdiction in federal court in the event of a formal dispute. Each element of the counter - notification requirement must be satisfied including the statement of good faith belief or else the service

---

[228]   A & M Records Inc. v. Napster Inc. 54 U.S. p.a. 2d (BNA) 11746 N.D.California, 2000.

[229]   Ibid.

[230]   OCILLA, 1998, Sec. 512(g)

provider will be ineligible for the safe harbor of the DMCA.[231] Upon receiving such a counter - notification, the service provider must send a copy to the party that originally the requested the removal. Unless that party then obtain a court order supporting removal if the material at issue, the service provider must restore access to the material between ten and fourteen days after receipt of counter - notification.[232]

To facilitate enforcement of the copyright owner's right to control access to his copyrighted work, the DMCA prohibits manufacturing or making available technologies, products and service used to defeat technological measurer controlling access.[233]

The procedure for handling the alleged infringements are as follows:

First, the copyright owner must officially notify the designated Agent, the Vice Chancellor of Information Technology, of the alleged infringement. Once effective notice is given, the Chief Information Officer will act expeditiously to remove or disable access to the material and promptly notify the affected user that their materials have been removed and blocked and notify the user of their counter notification rights.

If a counter notification is received from the user, the designated agent will provide a copy of the counter notification to the copyrights owner that sent the original notice. The copyright owner shall have seven business days to respond and indicate that they have failed a court action seeking to

---

[231] Perfect 10 Inc. v. Cybernet Ventures Inc. 213 F.Supp. 2d 1146 (C.D.Cal.2002).

[232] OCILLA, 1998, Sec. 512 (g) (2).

[233] DMCA, 1998, Section 1201 (a) (2) (b).

restrain the alleged infringement. If the designated agent does not receive such notice, the material must be unblocked or replaced within 10 to 14 business days of the receipt of the counter notification. In the event that a counter notification is not receive, infringement will be assumed as a matter of fact. In accordance with this policy, the Vice Chancellor of IT may impose limitations on continued use of computing resources by the infringer.

In the event that this is a second infringement by the same person, the individuals account privileges will be revoked, and the Vice - Chancellor for IT will undertake disciplinary review and legal action will be taken against the infringer. There are also certain sound practices to minimize the risk of infringement. They are:-

a) Do not use of works of unknown origin.
b) Obtain written permission from copyright owners.
c) Do not assume works are in public domain.
d) Do not assume "fair use" applies.
e) Do not put movies, videos, or music on a website.

Courts and legislation worldwide have dealt with the problems of online liability in different ways. Even so courts in United States and Europe have produced case law that is sometimes remarkably similar, is based on general principles of common or Europe civil tort law. Further, there are fundamental difference between the European and the United States solution in the scope of application. The European legislature opted for a horizontal approach whereas the United States has dealt with copyright liability within the frame work of the copyright law.

European Copyright Directive Implications

In 1977, the commission transmitted to the parliament and the council, a proposal for a European Parliament and Council Directive on the harmonization of certain aspects of Copyright and Related Rights in the Information Society. This marked the beginning of a legislative process for of the most extensively debated proposal in recent European Union history. After the European Parliament had examined the proposal in detail in it committees, it gave its opinion in the plenary session in favour of the proposal a amended. The Commission reacted with an amended proposal for a Directive, in which it endeavored to make Parliaments opinion into account as far as possible. After more than four years, the Directive was finally adopted in May, 2001. The Directive then has to be implemented by the Member states by bringing into force laws, regulations and administrative provisions necessary to comply with its content. The general objective of the Directive is to adapt legislation on copyright to new technologies, in particular the internet, and implement the internal obligations arising from the two WIPO Treaties at community level.

The ECD contains strong statements of copyright owner rights to control the reproduction, distribution and presentation of their works online. The ECD requires Legislative action by EC member States with respect to four rights: the reproduction right,[234] the communication to the public right,[235] the distribution right,[236] the protection against

---

[234]   European Copyright Directive, 2001, Article 2.
[235]   Ibid, Article 3.
[236]   Ibid, Article 4.

the circumvention[237] or abuse or electronic management and protection systems.[238]

With respect to the reproduction right, the ECD adopts essentially the same broad language of proposed Article 7(1) of the WCT that provoked so much controversy and was ultimately deleted from the WCT. The right provides the exclusive right to copyright owners to authorize or prohibit direct or indirect and temporary or permanent reproduction would seem to cover even ephemeral copies of a work made during the course of transmission or use of a copyrighted work in an online context. At the same it provides an explicit and automatic exemption for copies that are made incidental to the use of work through a technological process such as transmission through a network or loading into a memory for viewing or playing the works.[239] It is interesting to note that the majority of the exceptions to reproduction right are conditioned upon the right holders receiving fair compensation, they cover only copying that is for non- commercial purpose. Exception (b) is of particular interest, for it provides a right for natural persons to make copies for private use and for purposes that are neither directly nor indirectly commercial, provided the right holders receive fair compensation. Presumably, the exception would apply where a nature person has purchased a copy of copyrighted work. There by providing fair compensation to the right holders, and thereafter makes additional copies for personal and non commercial users. The drafters of the ECD deemed this right of private use to be such significance under

---

237   Ibid, Article 6.
238   Ibid, Article 7.
239   E.C.D., 2001, Article 5(1).

Article 6(4), Member States are permitted to take measures to ensure that beneficiaries of the right are able to take advantage of it, unless reproduction for private use has already been made possible right holders to the extent necessary to benefit from the exception or limitation concerned and in accordance with the provision of Article 5(2) (b) and(5), without preventing right holders from adopting adequate measure regarding the number of reproduction in accordance with these provisions. The Article 5(2) (b) is similar to Section 1008 of Audio and Home Recording Act of U.S.

In addition, the drafters of the ECD seemed to contemplate that intermediaries providing service through which infringing activities take place online should be subject to injective relief to stop unauthorized transmission of copyrighted works through its service. The ECD has provided an optional exception under Article 5(3) to the reproduction right and the right of communication to the public. This is applicable to those who are using copyrighted materials for teaching and purpose,[240] disabled persons used it for non commercial purposes,[241] making current copies[242] making criticism or review[243] public security and proceedings[244] political speeches and public lectures[245] religious and official celebrations[246] public works[247] incidental copying[248] public exhibition and

---

[240] Ibid, Article 5(3) (a).
[241] Ibid, Article 5(3) (b).
[242] Ibid, Article 5(3) (c).
[243] E.C.D., 2001, Article 5(3) (d).
[244] Ibid, Article 5 (3) (e).
[245] Ibid, Article 5(3) (f).
[246] Ibid, Article 5(3) (g).
[247] Ibid, Article 5(3) (h).
[248] Ibid, Article 5(3) (i).

sale[249] Caricature[250] demonstration or repair[251] reconstruction and making available for research or private study.

If the CD is implemented in U.K. Law then the permitted acts will no more possible. One of the optional permitted exceptions is that certain existing exceptions under a Member States Law may be permitted to continue. This exception is only permitted for non digital use of copyrighted works and material. It is not clear from the current proposals provided by the U.K patent Office whether this exception is utilized to permit fair dealing of works and materials by non digital use means for reached and private study but take the more limited and restricted approach required by the CD for digital means.

The ECD explicitly adopts both the right of communication to the public of copyrighted works and the right of making available to the public of fixed performances, by writ or wireless means, in language that parallels that of the WIPO performers and phonograms Treaty. The right of making available under Article 3(2) is actually boarder than the right required under Article 10 of the WPPT.

In total, the ECD explicitly grants a rights of transmission and access to copyrighted works and fixed performances, whereas the DMCA does not. It remains to be seen how broadly these rights mandated under the ECD will be adopted implementing legislation in EC Member Countries. However

---

[249]   Ibid, Article 5 (3) (j).
[250]   Ibid, Article 5(3) (k).
[251]   Ibid, Article 5 (3) (l).

this display between the express rights afforded under U.S. Law and the ECD raise considerable potential uncertainty. First, confusion is that, use of different language to denominate the various rights among countries may breed confusion. Second, differences of scope of the rights transmission and access are likely to arise between the United States and the EC virtue of the fact that these rights are spelled out as separate rights in the EC, whereas, if they exit at all, they are subsumed under a collection of various other rights in the United States. Adding further to the potential confusion is the possibility the some EC Member Countries may adopt these rights expressly, as mandated by the ECD, whereas the other countries may, like the United States, deem them to be subsumed in other rights already afforded under that country's laws. Because online transmission through the internet are inherently global, these disparities raise the possibilities that rights of varying scope will apply to an online transmission as it travels through computers in various countries, on the way to its ultimate destination. Similarly, legal rights of varying scope may apply depending upon in which the site of the access may arbitrary from a technical point of view, but significant from the legal point of view. Such a situation would not afford international uniformity that WIPO Treaties seek to establish.

The ECD adopts the approach of the DMCA, in that it outlawed both conduct and the manufacture or distribution of devices that could be used to defeat technological copyright protections. With respect to conduct, Article 6(1) provides that Member States shall provide adequate legal protection against the circumvention of any effective technological measures, which the person concerned carries out in the knowledge or with reasonable grounds to know that he or she is pursuing that objective. The language of Article 6(1) includes a knowledge requirement that is not expressly presented in the prohibition of section 1202 (a) (1) (A) of the DMCA. But unlike the DMCA, there are no enumerated exceptions to the ban on circumvention in the ECD. Like the DMCA, the ECD does not require that the circumvention of the technical measures be done for the purpose of facilitating or engaging in an act of infringement. With respect to the manufacture or distribution of devices that could be used to defeat technological copyright protections. Article 6(2) provides that Member State shall provide adequate legal protection against the manufacture, import, distribution, sale, rental, advertisement for sale or rental or possession for commercial purposes of devices, products or components or the provision of services which:

a) Are promoted, advertised or marketed for the purpose of circumvention, or

b) Have only a limited commercially significant purpose or use other than to circumvent, or,

c) Are primarily designed, produced, adapted or performed for the purpose of enabling or facilitating the circumvention of, any effective technological measures.

The forgoing three criterion are very similar to the criteria enumerated in the prohibition of technology, devices and service contained in sections 1201(a) (2) and 1201 (b) of the DMCA. However by prohibiting preparatory activities no circumvention, Article 6 (2) goes further than the WCT requires.

One possible difference between the ECD and DMCA may lie in the scope of what types of technological measures are prohibited from circumvention. Specifically, the prohibitions of the

DMCA are expressly directed toward technology, devices and services that circumvent technological measures that effectively control access to a copyrighted work and protect rights of copyright holders. By contrast, the definition of technological measures in the ECD, at first glance, sees directed only toward protecting rights of a copyright holder, and not restricting access. Article 6(3) defines the expression technological measures to mean to prevent or restrict acts, in respect of works or the subject matter, which are not authorized by the right holders of any copyright or any right related to copyright.

However, the concept of access control seems to come in to ECD indirectly through the definition of effective control. Specifically, Article 6(3) provides that technological measures is controlled by right holders through application of an access control or protection process such as encryption, scrambling or other transformation of the work or other subject matter or a copy control mechanism, which achieves the measures and effective, it appears that the ECD effectively prohibits the circumvention of technological measures that both control access and that project the rights of a copyright holder just as does the DMCA.

In regard to Article 6(4) of the Directive, the U.K. implementation enables beneficiaries of exception under Article 5(2) (a), 2(c), 2(d), 2(e), 3(a) or 3(e) of the Directive to appeal to the Secretary of State where a technological measures prevent them from benefiting from these exceptions. The Secretary of State may issue directions enabling the complaint to benefit from the exception concerned even though he is not obliged to do so.

Librarians and archivists are simply impeded, if they must appeal to the Secretary of State and every occasion that they need to reproduce a copy of a work protected by some copy protection system. Archivists might except to need to this on receipt of practically every copy protected work they receive, since they will need to ensure that have an unprotected copy that will remain accessible once the work passes out of copyright.

The scope of Article 7 is potentially narrower than that of the DMCA. The prohibitions of Article 7(1) are all expressly directed to electronic rights management information. In addition, the commentary states that Article 7 aims only at the protection of electronic rights management and does not cover all kinds of information that could be attached to the protected material as in the case of DMCA provisions.

Comparison of OCILLA with E-Commerce Directive.

The liability regime of the Electronic Commerce Directive has been largely inspired by the DMCA. However, there are a few intriguing differences between the two instruments. Contrary to the Directive, which treats liability issues horizontally, the DMCA deals only with liability for copyright infringement. Unlike the European Copyright Directive, the Act is silent on the copyright status of caching as such. Like the Electronic Commerce Directive the DMCA does not deal with the matter in terms of substantive law, but merely sets certain standards of online intermediary liability. From the provider perspective, this approach has the advantage that he is made immune from both direct and liability, whereas if proxy catching were merely an exempted Act, a provider might still incur liability for contributory infringement.

Unlike the E-Commerce Directive the DMCA does not totally ruled out a duty to monitor. In the future, such a duty may arise if technologies become available that facilitate the monitoring of the transmitted, cached or hosted content, and if implementing these technologies imposes on the provider neither substantial costs nor substantial burden on his systems. The DMCA goes a step further than the E- Commerce Directive, in that it provided for extensive notice and take down procedure. Under the Act a hosting service provider must take down or remove material if he receives a notification of infringement. The E-Commerce Directive does not set a similar condition to escape liability. Even so, European Courts might find, on the basis of general principles of law, that the provider has actual knowledge of the material being taken down at the originating source on notification of such removal, and thus be held liable if cached copy is not expeditiously blocked. Consequently, a European notification may play an important role as well.

Chapter IV

Theories of Liabilty for Infringement of Author's Rights In Internet

Like the traditional copyright infringement there is liability due to the posting or uploading of materials on the Internet, if such posting or uploading is without the permission of the copyright owner. The digital treaties only outline the minimum level protection that should be given and they no were deals with infringement matters or liability issues. However, in the case of piracy, the greatest problem may not be identifying whether or not an originator of material has infringed copyright, but identifying who and where the originator is. Liabilities of Internet service providers, network operators etc. Which arguably infringes copyright of others have greatest concern here.

Network operators that carry bits of data containing infringing material, along the route of transmission may be liable for infringement of copyright in cyberspace. Even though there are good policy reasons not to hold network operators liable for secondary infringement, many of which have actively drawn to the attention of legislators by network operators themselves. The service providers are constantly being dragged into and harassed in litigations, and being accused for no reason at all.[252] This is the result of non - formulation of specific or generic liability in many countries. In many cases of copyright infringement, it can be found that, the copy is not being made accessible by the Internet access providers, but by the end user.[253] The court on the basis of the facts and circumstances of the individual cases has arrived at varying conclusions.

There are three types of copyright infringement, namely, direct copyright infringement, contributory infringement and vicarious infringement.

Direct Infringement

Direct copyright infringement takes place when the exclusive rights of the copyright owner are violated.[254] That is when a person does any of the acts which fall within exclusive rights of the copyright owner. Direct infringement does not require knowledge of the fact that an infringement is occurring. Infringer does not even need to know that the work is copyrighted. Simply copying the work makes the person liable for copyright infringement.

Direct infringement is a strict liability tort. Even innocent copying of the work may include, innocently receiving an e-mail that is an infringement of the copyright of another, and

---

[252] Religious Technology Center v. Netcom Online Communication Services, 907 F.Supp. 1361..

[253] That is, the Internet access providers are positively not publishing as they do not edit, nor add to the text.

[254] U.S. Copyright Act, 1976, Sec. 106.

then subsequently printing that e- mail message to hard copy form. Further, if storage of images in RAM of a computer is determined to be copying for the purpose of copyright law. Then simply browsing the Internet would amount to innocent infringement.

In infringement action, a plaintiff is required to prove ownership of the copyright and copying by the defendant.[255] Proof of a defendant's intention to infringement is not an element of plaintiff's case.[256] A defendant cannot escape from liability on the grounds of unconscious copying or based on a work that of a third person who has, in fAct, unlawfully copied from another. Similarly a publisher cannot escape from liability simply by publishing infringing material provided by a third party. Therefore the direct copyright infringement offers the copyright owner the ability to hold a particular party liable without any proof of intent, violation of knowledge etc. from their part.[257]

The first case which violation focused mainly on the distinction between direct and indirect liability. All cases that have been decided prior to the enactment of the safe harbors provisions of the DMCA[258], addressed mainly on the online service provider's liability for direct infringement. It should be noted that, even if a service provider falls outside a DMCA

---

[255] Sid and Marty Kroft Television Productions v. McDonald's Corporation, 562 F.2d. 1157, 1162, 9th Cir, 1977.

[256] Costello publication co. v. Rostelle, 670 F.2d. 1035, 1044 D.C. Circuit, 1981.

[257] U.S. Copyright Act, 1976, Sec. 106.

[258] OCILLA, 1998, Sec. 512.

safe harbor, its conduct still may not rise to the level of direct infringement.[259]

In a prominent case, the situation was that, Netcom, the internet service provider, Erlich, a Netcom subscriber and Klemesured, BBS operator were used by Religious Technology Center alleging copyright infringement. The allegation was that the Erlich's posting RTC's copyrighted material on the BBS was illegal. Here plaintiff argued that Netcom and BBS operator found themselves in this because, Erlich used their computer facilities to publish unauthorized copies of the plaintiff's copyrighted work in an Internet news group, scientology. The defendant OSP's contention was that, they were the mere temporary host of messages posted to newsgroups and hence they could not be made liable for direct copyright potentially liable of its large number of users to unlimited tort liability. But the defendant BBS operator's contention was that, the infringing copies stored in a defendant system and then retransmitted to other server will not make direct copyright infringement.

Therefore the court held that the OSP and the BBS operator were not liable, because of the reason that, Netcom's act if implementing a system, which automatically and uniformly created temporary copies of all data set through it was not like that of the owner of copying machine who allow the public made copies with it.[260] Therefore the service provider has no direct liability for user postings.

---

[259] Costar Group, Inc. v. Loopnet Inc. 2004 U.5.App. LEXIS 12123, 19-28.

[260] Religious Technology Center v. Netcom Online Communication Services, 907. F.Supp. N.D.California, 1995,.1361.

The same view was taken by the court in another case.[261] In this case Sega Enterprises used the BBS and its operator Chad Sherman who solicited the infringement of Sega's copyrighted videogames on to the BBS. Here the defendant permitted its subscribers to upload and download the videogames.[262] The court refused to impose direct liability on BBS, by citing the Netcom case and held that, even though copyright is a strict liability status, there should be some element of volition or causation which is lacking where a defendant's system were merely used to create a copy by a third party.[263]

Another case also reiterated the same ratio.[264] In this case the defendant Sebella was the system operator of a BBS, which contained a directory, through which uploading and downloading of infringing copies of Sega's videogames is possible. Moreover the defendant sold copiers that enabled users to play Sega games directly by using floppy disks without the need for a Sega game cartridge and allowed purchasers to download files from her BBS without charge for a certain period of time. By adopting the view in Netcom case, the court held that even though the defendant's activities were more than participatory than those of the defendant in Netcom, Sebella is not directly liable because, has no bearing on whether Sebella directly caused the copying to occur.[265] Here

---

[261] Sega Enterprises Ltd v. MAPHIA, 948. F.Supp. 679, N.D.California, 1996.

[262] Sega Enterprises Ltd v. MAPHIA, 948. F.Supp. 679, N.D.California, 1996.

[263] Ibid.

[264] Sega Enterprises Ltd v. Sabella, 948. F.Supp. 648, N.D.California. 1996.

[265] Ibid.

Sebella knew her BBS user's were infringing the plaintiff's copyright or encouraged them to do so by providing privilege to downloading and sold copiers etc.[266] Hence this decision is liable to a criticism because the escaping from direct liability is upon a weak point.

Several cases were decided in contrast to the preceding cases, because of the reason that the defendant BBS operator has a more direct participation in the infringing activities of its users and subscribes. In a case,[267] George Frena operated a BBS through which subscribers can view photographs and download them into their computer. One subscriber of the defendant uploaded files containing pictures from the play boy magazine.[268] The defendant had no knowledge of the infringing activities and had not remove such photographs as he became aware of it. Accordingly, the court found liability in Frena's activity even though he is not directly participating in the infringing activities.[269] Hence it was held that Frena's intention is irrelevant and concluded that he is liable for supplying a product containing unauthorized copies of the copyrighted works.

The court confirmed this stand in another case,[270] where the defendant web world operated a website. Which made adult images available to subscribers payment of certain amount for a

---

[266] Ibid.

[267] Playboy Enterprises Inc. v. Frena, 839 F.Supp. 648. N.D.California, 1996.

[268] Ibd.

[269] Playboy Enterprises Inc. v. Frena, 839 F.Supp. 648. N.D.California, 1996.

[270] Playboy Enterprises v. Webbworld, 968 F.Supp. 1171. N.D. Texas, 1997.

period. Here the images became available through the website which were originally created by or for the plaintiff's Playboy Enterprises Inc. The defendant contended that, under the logic of Netcom case, it could not be held directly liable for copyright infringement. The court differentiated the Netcom case from this case on the ground that the former did not create or control of information available to its subscribers, but only provide access to the Internet. In contradiction to the former case, here the website receiving payment for selling the images and therefore acting as more than merely an information conduit and so liable for direct copyright infringement.[271] In another case[272] also, the BBS operator who encouraged uploading and who screened files before making them publicly available were held liable for direct and contributory copyright infringement for violating owner's rights of distribution and public display.

The court in another case[273] held that, because the defendant authorized the third party to upload files to his site, the defendant was directly liable for such uploading. It act as a violation of the exclusive right under the copyright status to authorize others to reproduce the copyrighted work.[274]

The position in another case[275] is that, direct infringement is on the ISP host of website, which contained infringing

---

[271] Ibid.

[272] Playboy Enterprises v. Russ Hardenburgh 982 F.Supp. 503. N.D. Ohio 1997.

[273] Playboy Enterprises v. Sanfilippo, 1998 U.S. Dist. LEXIS 5125, S.D. California, 1998.

[274] U.S. Copyright Act, 1976, Sec. 106.

[275] Marobic FL Inc. v. National Association of Fire Equipment Distributors, 45 U.S.P.Q 2d. 1236, ND. 111. 1997.

material because ISP engaged in direct violation of the both the plaintiff's distribution right and public display right. The court concluded that mere making available of the files for downloading was sufficient for liability, because, once the files were uploaded, they were available for down loading by Internet users and the server transmitted the files to some internet users when requested.[276]

In another case[277] the court has taken a very strict view, in which Los Angeles Times and Washington post filed copyright infringement lawsuit against a website operator. This site contained news stories from many source and allowed its users to attach comments on it. The fair use argument is rejected by the court and held that there is liability for such infringement.[278] The court adopted the same ratio in another case.[279] The Recording Industry Association of America filed a complaint alleging infringement against MP.3 services, which allowed users to gain access through the Internet and download digital copies of commercial CDs. The court considered it as a prima case of direct copyright infringement and rejected the defendant's fair use defence.

But contrastingly, in another cases court refused the direct infringement liability of OSPs on the ground that the infringing materials are posted on their services without their knowledge,

---

[276] Marobic FL Inclusive v. National Association of Fire Equipment Distributors, 45 U.S.P.Q 2d. N.D.111. 1997.

[277] Los Angeles Times v. Free Republic, 54 U.S.P.Q. 2d 1453, C.D. California, 2000.

[278] Ibid.

[279] MP3. Com Inc v. UMG Recordings Inc. No.00 Civ. 0472, SDNY, January 21, 2000.

In one case,[280] a commercial real estate listing service hosted infringing photographs of property and in another case[281] it was fictional works. Once again it was reflected in another case,[282] where the court refused to hold the defendant liable as a direct copyright infringer, based on the unauthorized presence of plaintiff's copyrighted photographs on its several member sites.

To conclude, Internet Service Provider is not a direct infringer because of the reason that they only owns an electronic facility that responds to the user's input.[283] The ISPs should not be held liable as a copier by the view that, the concept of copying requires fixation for more than a transitory duration.[284]

Contributory Liability

In an on line activity, if the service provider is not directly liable, the next step is to determine whether they are contributory liable. Contributory liability is based on the principle that, a party may be liable for contributory infringement where with the knowledge of infringing activity, it induces causes of

---

[280] Costar v. Loopnet, 164 F.Supp. 2d. 1051, C.D. California, 2002.

[281] Elhson v. Robertson, 189 F.Supp. 2d. 1051, C.D. California, 2002.

[282] Perfect 10 v. Cybernet Ventures Inc., 213 F.Supp. 2d 1146, C.D. California, 2002.

[283] Karl. S Kaplan, Why do we protect Intellectual property?, Cyber Law Journal, 31. Dec. 1998.

[284] Bruce. A. Lehman, Information Infrastructure Task Force, Working group on Intellectual Property Rights, September 1995.

materially contribute to the infringing activity of another.[285] Thus person who induce others to infringe copyright shall be of guilty contributory infringement.

For liability, there must be direct infringement to which the contributory infringer has knowledge and encouraged or facilitated.[286] As a judicial tool, the purpose of contributory liability is to empower copyright owners to use the root cause of numerous infringements rather than suing many individual for direct infringement.[287]

The requirement of knowledge means actual and constructive knowledge.[288] This requirement may eliminate the contributory liability of ISP's or BBS operator by the reason that, they are merely a passive information conduit and has no knowledge of the infringement.[289] However, a number of cases suggest that ISPs cannot simply continue to provide the facility to enable infringement.

In a case,[290] the court concluded that, unauthorized uses of a copyright is not an infringement unless it conflicts with one of the specific exclusive rights conferred by the copyright statute. Thus the court held that if a product is capable of other

---

[285] Cable/Home Communication Corporation v. Net Work Production Inc., 902 F. 2d 829-845, 11th circuit, 1990.

[286] Costella v. Morris, 820 F. 2d. 362, 365 11th circuit, 1987.

[287] Moye J.M, How Sony Survived: peer to peer software, Grokster, and contributory copyright liability in the twenty first century, North Carolina Law Review, 84 (2006) 646.

[288] A & M Records Inc. v. Napster Inc. 239 F 3d 1004.

[289] Graves T, Picking up the piece of Grokster: A New approach to file – sharing, Hastings communications & Entertainment Law Journal, 27 (2004) 28.

[290] Sony Corporation of America v. Universal City Studios Inc. 464U.S. 1984.

non-infringing and substantially lawful uses the producer could not be liable and hence Sony could not be held liable for contributory infringement. Operator could be made liable for contributory infringement.

The issue in a case[291] was that the ISP and BBS operator could be made liable for contributory infringement on the basis that they had the of knowledge and they provide access to the distribution of the copyrighted material. Netcom's contention here was that to be held liable for infringement, it must have the knowledge of the infringed activity and materially participated in it, but it did not have such knowledge as required by the court for holding it contributory liable for the acts of another. Further Netcom simply served as a passive transmitter. The fact that Netcom was just one of dozens of access providers throughout the country shows the immateriality of its contribution to the other defendant's conduct and hence not liable for this infringement. But the BBS operator's argument is that, for making them contributorily liable it should have to establish that they solicited or encouraged the infringing activities. But the information service was less directly involved in creating unauthorized copies and so not liable. So the court held that Netcom may be liable for contributory infringement by the reason of its failure to cancel the infringing materil and there by stop an infringing copy from being distributed throughout the world. It may constitute substantial participation the infringing activity.[292] However, the court noted it carefully that where an operator was an operator was unable to verify

---

[291] Religious Technology Center v. Netcom Online Communication Services, 907 F.Supp. 1361, N.D.California, 1995.
[292] Ibid.

the cliam infringement because of the lack of knowledge is a reasonable ground for avoiding contributory infringement.

The same issue was in consideration in another case.[293] The plaintiff by citing the 9th circuit decision[294] argued that BBS and its operator had participated in infringement an d had the clear knowledge about infringement. It was established by Sega that unauthorized copies of the video game are also made when they are downloaded. Copying was facilitated and encouraged by the BBS, to make such additional copies by users. Even if the defendants do not know exactly when the games it will be uploaded to or downloaded from the BBS, their role in the copying direction, knowledge and encouragement amounts to contributory infringement. For this purpose, the court also cited the Ninth Circuit Court decision[295] for the proposition that providing facilities for known infringing activities were sufficient to show contributory liability.

It remarkable case[296] the court ruled in favour of the plaintiff and held that, to fix the liability of contributory infringement, there was no need of actual knowledge and the defendant materially contribute to the infringing activity.

---

[293] Sega Enterprises v. MAPHIA, 948 F.Supp., 923, N.D.California, 1996.

[294] Fonovisa Inc. v. Cherry Auction Inc. 76 F.3d 259, 9th cicuit, 1996.

[295] Fonovisa Inc. v. Cherry Auction Inc. 76 F.3d 259, 9th circuit 1996.

[296] RIAA v. Napster, 114 F.Supp. 2d 896, N.D.California, 2000.

Another case challenged the legality of the peer to peer file sharing.[297] In this case the plaintiff's include several leading motion picture studios, record companies and music publishers who filed a copyright infringement against Scour Inc. Unlike the Nepster service, which was limited to the exchange of both music files in MP3 formal,[298] the Score Inc. enabled the peer to peer exchange of both music and motion picture files among the hard drives of Score users. Abanner is established by the scour website containing a top five search list for Score users, who frequently requesting for current motion picture title and music recordings. On allegation, Score Inc. announced that in order to facilitate a copyright Infringement Ligigation it would shut down its exchange service and offer the sale of its assets.

The same view was pointed out in another case.[299] In this case Aimster enabled its members for a certain amount of fee to download with a single click around 40 songs most oftenly shared by Aimster users and those were invariable copyrighted by the plaintiff's was enough to establish liability for contributory infringement.[300] Another case[301] addressed in detail the knowledge of an OSP had duty to prevent repeat infringements in the future if the OSP had a notice of the

---

[297] P 2 P transfers directly from the computer of one user to the computer of another user without passing through the Napster service.

[298] MP3 is an algorithm that compresses a digital musical file where reducing the size of the file so that it more easily and quickly can be downloaded over the internet.

[299] Re Aimster copyright Litigation, 252 F.Supp. 2d 634 N.D. 111, 2002.

[300] Re Aimster copyright Litigation, 252 F.Supp. 2d 634 N.D. 111, 2002,

[301] Costar v. Loopnet, 164 F.Supp. 2d 688. D. M.D. 2001.

going infringement. The plaintiff here should have to establish that the notice it gave to the OSP complied the contructive knowledge of specific infringing activity.

The court refused to hold an OSP liable because of the fact they did not have the actual knowledge.[302] But yet another case found liability in OSP.[303] In the case the court found that Cybernet had knowledge of the infringements and the Cybernet's site reviewers every site before allowing them to became its members. The court here found that upon evidence there was many sites contained disclaimers to the effect that the site did not held copyrights for the works on the site.[304] Therefore it was ruled that perfect 10 had established a strong likelihood of success in the contributory infringements claim.[305]

In another recent case[306], the California District Court distinguished the services at issue in Napster and Aimster from Kazaa nad Gnutella peer to peer software and refused to hold defendants liable for contributory infringements. The court stated that in Grokster case, defendants distributed products, but did not provide services same as Nepster or Aimster. The court noted that the software capable of non- infringing uses, but did not inquired as to the substantiality or commercial siginificance of those uses. It also asked whether actual knowledge of specific infringement accrued at a time when

---

[302] Ellison v. Robertson, 189 F.Supp. 2d 1051. C.D. California 2002.

[303] Perfect 10 Inc. v. Cybernet Ventures Inc. 213 F.Supp. 2d. 1051, C.D. California, 2002.

[304] Ibid.

[305] Ibid, p. 1162.

[306] MGM studios Inc. v. Grokster Ltd. 259 F.Supp. 2d..

defendants martially contributed to the alleged infringements, and could therefore do something about it[307]. Accordingly to the extent that defendants distributed products rather than provided service, they were in the position of companies and an action for contributory infringements could not lie because there was no evidence of defendants active and substantial contribution to the infringement itself.[308] for such a decision the court placed its reliance mainly on the Sony case.[309]

The matter went on appeal to the Supreme court, which overturned the decision of lower courts and held the P2P networks liable for contributory infringement.[310] The court in this regard stated that nothing in Sony requires courts to ignore evidence of intent to promote infringement if such evidence exist.[311] According to the court, the practical alternative in case of infringement is to go against the distributor of copying device for secondary liability on a theory of contributory or vicarious infringement.[312] Thus the U.S. Supreme Court made a decision which attempted to steer a technologists.[313]

---

[307]   Ibid, p. 1043

[308]   MGM studios Inc. v. Grokster Ltd. 259 F.Supp. 2d. p. 1043

[309]   Sony Corporation of America v. Universal City studios Inc. 464 U.S 417 1984.

[310]   MGM studios Inc. v. Grokster Ltd, 125 S ct 2764 2005.

[311]   Ibid.

[312]   Ibid. p. 2776.

[313]   Chen R.G., Rewinding Sony: An inducence theory of secondary liability (2005) European Intellectual Property Review, 27 (11) (2005) 428.

Vicarious Liability

Vicarious liability is a doctrine where a third party may be liable for the infringement act of another if such third party, has the right and ability to control the infringing act of another and receives a direct financial benefit from the infringement.[314] Unlike contributory infringement, knowledge is not an element of vicarious liability.[315]

The court refused to apply on Netcom under the vicarious liability theory.[316] In this case the court found that there was a genuine issue of material fact as to whether Netcom had the right and ability to control the activities of its subscribers. It was of the view that Netcom could identify posting containing particular words or from particular individuals by an easy software modification. And about thousand occasions Netcom had acted to suspend its subscribers account.

Even though, the court noted that, the second point of the requirement was not fulfilled here because there was no evidence to show that Netcom a direct financial benefit from the alleged postings or that such postings enhanced the value of its service to subscribes. New subscribes also not attracted by such postings.[317]

---

[314] Shapiro Bernstein and co. v. H.L.Green Co. 326 F. 2d. 304, second circuit, 1963.

[315] Religious Technology Center v. Netcom Online Communication Services 907. F.Supp. 1361, N.D.California, 1995.

[316] Ibid.

[317] Religious Technology Center v. Netcom Online Communication Services, 907 F.Supp. 1361 N.D.California, 1995.

But the court refused to adopt the same view in another case.[318] The court found that Napster has ability to block its users about whom right holder complaint was tantamount to an admission that defendant can, and sometimes does, police its service.[319] Here the court held that even if the defendant is capable of supervisory powers, it need not exercise such power.. The plaintiff's had shown a reasonable likelihood that Napster had a direct financial benefit in the infringing activity and attracted and many users by offering an increasing amount of quality music for free of charge. The court found a similar situation of direct financial interest, which is sufficient for vicarious liability in another case[320]. Thus it was held that on the vicarious infringement claim, the plaintiff's argument was successful.[321]

In another case[322] also the court reiterated liability in which it was held that the defendant Cyber net had a direct financial interest in the infringing activities of its member sites. Moreover they attracted new subscribers to its service. The court also noted that Cyber net and its member site acted as a single brand and the subscribers paid all the money for their subscription fees directly to Cyber net, which then handover it as commission to the member site.[323] So it can be concluded that Cyber net had the ability to control its member sites.

---

[318] RIAA v. Napster, 114 F.Supp. 2d. 896, M.D. California, 2002.

[319] Ibid, p. 921.

[320] Fonovisa Inc. v. Cherry Auction Inc. 76 F. 3d. 259 9th circuit, 1990.

[321] RIAA v. Napster, 114 F.Supp. 2d. M.D. California, 2000, p. 921-922.

[322] Perfect 10 Inc. v. Cybernet Ventures Inc. 45. U.S.P.Q 2d, 1236, N.O.111, 1997.

[323] Ibid, p. 1171-1172.

Accordingly the court held that to be vicariously liable, Cyber net had enough control over the infringing activity.[324]

In another case[325] also the court similarly ruled that Aimster had the right and ability to supervise its users because it retained the right under its terms of service to terminate its service to the users for repeated violation. Thus the Aimster enjoyed sufficient control and direct financial benefit for the purpose of vicarious liability.[326] Another recent case[327] also reiterated the same standard.

Earlier position is that, vicarious liability cannot be considered as an appropriate standard because the access provider does not maintain an agency relationship with the bulletin board subscriber. The insufficiency of the relationship between the access provider and the subscriber illustrates the vicarious liability as not a viable solution. Access providers will only be held liable, when they have notice of the ongoing infringement. In some instance, the access provider may be indirectly related to the infringement, but is no way related to the infringement[328]. This standard protects both the copyright holder's and the access providers interest without destroying the goals and rights of the parties.

Intermediary Liability under DMCA

Copyright protection in the United States emanates from the Constitution itself. It is the first document that authorized

---

[324] Ibid, p.1173.

[325] Re Aimster Copyright Litigation, 252 F.Supp. N.D. 111, 2002.

[326] Ibid.

[327] MGM studios Inc. v. Grokster Ltd, 125 S Ct 2764 2005

[328] Cubby v. Compuserve, 776 F.Supp. 135 SDNY 1999.

the Congress to promote the progress of science and other useful arts and thereby enshrined exclusive protection to the authors and inventors with respect to their work.[329] Pursuant to this they enacted United States Copyright Act, 1976 and Digital Millennium Copyright Act, 1998.

The United States doctrine of contributory Infringement is based on the basic common law doctrine that one who knowingly participate or furthers a tortuous act is jointly and severally liable with the prime tort feasors[330] and thus the defendant must have the knowledge of the Infringement and have induced, caused or materially a contributed to the third party's Infringing conduct.[331]

So the United States Congress in 1998 codified the Online Copyright Infringement liability Act under DMCA[332]. The purpose behind this safe harbor is to provide to those entities that qualify as network systems providers, federal immunization from claims brought against them by copyright owner based on a theory of secondary liability.

Search engines and ISPs etc. With multiple links to third parties provide network access to subscribers and who may post materials that infringing copyright. In that capacity the customers are direct infringer's violating the copyright owner's exclusive statutory rights to reproduce the work and so the direct infringer is held primarily liable for the Infringement. Exemption from secondary liability

---

[329] U.S. Constitution, Art 1, Sec. 8, Clause 8.

[330] Screen Gems-Columbia Music Inc. v. Mark Pi. Records Inc. 256 FSupp. 399 (SDNY, 1966).

[331] Gershwin Publishing Corp. v. Columbia Artists Management Inc. 443 F. 2d 1159. 2d Cir. 1971.

[332] OCILLA, 1998, Sec. 512.

Under the tort theories of contributory Infringement and vicarious liability, copyright law also allows claims against secondary infringers. These theories of secondary copyright Infringement become a significant copyright claim in view of the function of online service providers. So long as the online service providers are in compliance with the DMCA by using proper notification of its policy regarding alleged copyright Infringement and establishing a company agent to be notified in the event of such Infringement, they are exempt from secondary liability. This does not mean that entities such as search engines, Internet service providers, website etc. With multiple links can be casual about this exemption. Strict compliance with the DMCA[333] provision is an important function of copyright management by such entities. If the entity qualify for the DMCA safe harbor exemption, only the direct infringer will be held liable for copyright damages.[334] But the court should have to look into whether the service providers provided an integral service to the infringer for facilitating the Infringement[335] or they were just a passive conduit for the Infringing activity.

United States apex court, when deciding a case[336] disregarded with the fact that the copyright laws are rather archaic in nature and not updated according to the changing technology. A balance has to struck between the conflicting interests of protection and innovation.

---

[333]   Ibid.

[334]   Ferrera, Lichtenstein, Reder, Bird, Schiano, Cyber Law- Text & Cases, second Ed. 2003, Thomson, p. 103.

[335]   A & M Records. Inc. v. Napster Inc. 239 F 3d 1004. P. 1002.

[336]   MGM studios Inc. v. Grokster Ltd, 125 S Ct 2764 2005.

Indian Scenario

The owner of a copyright has a civil remedy[337] against any person who infringes the copyrighted work. However, such a remedy is not subject to a direct Infringement or contributory Infringement. It merely provides as the right of copyright owner to claim damages, injunction or accounts of profits any Infringes his copyright.

However, if any person Infringes or abets t o such Infringement, then in that case, all such persons would be held criminally liable for such acts.[338]

The test of direct and contributory Infringement has not been dealt with in very expressive terms. However, it charges a person with criminal liability who abets such crime. Though the copyright Act does not define such abetment, it is provided by Indian penal Code as an offence.[339]

Moreover, it is evident that no specific provision exists with regard to contributory Infringement, it can be included along with direct Infringement[340]. Even though it primarily refers to direct copyright Infringement, it says that any person without a license, who permits for profit any place to be used for communication of the work to the public will be held liable.[341] Such a liberal interpretation can be construed to include contributory Infringement cases. For contributory

---

[337] Indian Copyright Act, 1957, Sec. 55
[338] Ibid, Sec. 63.
[339] Indian Penal Code, 1860, Sec. 107.
[340] Indian Copyright Act, 1957, Sec. 51 (a) (ii)
[341] Sneha Jha, An Analysis of the Theory of Contributory Infringement, Journal of Intellectual Property Rights, Vol. 11, September 2006, p. 318-325.

Infringement, intention is an essential component and a person who allows the usage for communication of the work for profit, necessarily has the intent to commit the wrong.

The Information Technology Act provides that network service providers would not be held liable in certain cases.[342] Due to this section the service provider has no liability for any third party Infringement, if it proves that the offence was committed without his knowledge and had exercised all due diligence to prevent such commission of offence. Neither the IT Act nor the Copyright Act makes express mention of the liability of the service provider for copyright Infringement.

When considering the Napster case in Indian Position, though the activities of Napster would not amount to direct copyright Infringement, it may be possible to argue that Napster facilities unauthorized copying and hence, should be liable for contributory and vicarious Infringement. It may be based on a proposition that in a case[343] the Indian courts have held that showing of video films over a cable network amounts to broadcasting or communicating it to a section of the public. The Honorable Supreme Court also held that such broad casting directly affected the earnings of the author and violated his intellectual property rights. The case also held that assisting in infringement would amount to the Infringement of copyright.

No Napster would not be able to claim immunity under the network service provider provision of the Indian Information Technology Act, as the provision stipulates that a network

---

[342]   Indian Information Technology Act, 2000, Sec. 79.
[343]   Garware Plastic and Polyester Ltd. V. Telelink, A.I.R 1989 Bom. 331.

provider can claim immunity against third party information only and here the violation is by the Napster subscribers. It has to prove that the contravention was committed without his knowledge, or that he had exercised all Due Diligence to prevent the commission of such an offence or contravention. Napster is not only aware of such contravention, but is also facilitating it by actively supplying the software and service to its subscribers that makes such a contravention possible.

In most jurisdiction, in situations where ISPs are transmitting information to and from third parties and are hosting information for that particular purpose, there appears to be growing consensus amongst legislators and judges that they should not be held absolutely liable for breaches of the law committed by their users. Hence liability is tending to be imposed in circumstances where (a) the IPS knows or has reason to believe that the information content it is transmitting is unlawful (b) regardless of the ISPs knowledge, it benefits directly from the transmission and (c) the ISP fails to take reasonable steps to determine if the information content transmits is unlawful. Therefore as held in Grokster case[344] a balance has to struck between the conflicting interests of protection and innovation.

---

[344] MGM studios Inc. v. Grokster Ltd, 125 S Ct 2764, 2005.

CHAPTER V

Limitations on Copyright Owner's Exclusive Rights and Remedies for Infrigement

Infringement of copyright is permissible under certain socially desirable circumstances[345].

A copyright work can be used without the consent of the copyright holder to facilitate education, research and dissemination of knowledge and information[346] so as to promote economic and cultural growth of the society. But there is a possibility that the operation of exception may come to be excluded In the online environment, which is often referred to as the digital lock -up and this had attracted considerable attention from commentators over recent years.[347]

---

[345] WCT, 1996, Art. 10

[346] CCH Canadian v. Law Society of Upper Canada, 2004, SCC, 13.

[347] T. Brogan, Fair use No Longer: How the DMCA Bars Fair Use of Digitally Stored Works (2002) 16 Saint John's Journal of Legal Commentary, 691.

Every country has some kind of defences available in their copyright laws. Indian Copyright Act contains elaborate provisions identifying limitations and exceptions to the rights[348], which may be possible to extend into digital environment.

1. De Minimis

It is defence granted to those users who use the work for a very short of time or who use such work in the least expensive way, such as to cause no or very little harm to the copyright holder. In a case,[349] the plaintiff alleged that the headlines copied by the defendant on to his site formed literary works. However, the defendant stated that a small number of words cannot be qualified as literary works and thus the use of such words stands de minims. However, the court rejected the defendant's arguments and held the defendant liable for copyright Infringement.

De minimis is a good defence available to the users who cache material from copyrighted work to the RAM or hard disk. Storage of work in RAM or hard disk of the user's personal computer hardly affects the owner's rights in the work. However, the use of such stored work for further exploitation cannot be claimed as de minimis. De minimis also generally not granted to the Internet service providers for caching[350]. In the case of ISP caching, there is the possibility of use of the work by some other user. Such use would cause

---

[348]   Indian Copyright Act, 1957, Sec. 52.
[349]   Shetland Times v. Dr. Jonathan Wills, 1997 FSR 304.
[350]   Pankaj Jain & Pandey Sangeet Rai, Copyright and Trademark laws relating to computers, Eastern Book co., 2005. P. 74.

a loss to the copyright owner. But if there is a situation where the courts find that the material cached is not in the control of ISPs, then in such cases they should not be made responsible.

2. Ignorance

Ignorance of law is no excuse. However, the defence of ignorance usually assists the infringer in reducing the quantum of damages to be paid. Applicability of this defence sometimes plays a major role in case of copyright Infringement in Internet. Ignorance is a defence applicable in cases where there are no basic norms or rules set up still date to distinguish between what is right and what is wrong[351]. Hence, in cyber laws where there is no proper formulation of laws, people usually plead the defence of ignorance.

3. Fair use

Doctrine of fair use is a long standing equitable doctrine that aims at guarding against both over or under production of information relative to the social optimum level of protection. The socially optimal level of protection could be defined as that, which provides the owner of the right with just and enough incentive to invest in the particular activity while leaving the public with sufficient information from which further progress may result.[352]

---

[351] Ibid.
[352] Ann Bartow Educational fair use in Copyright: Reclaiming the Right to Photocopy Freely Uni. Pitt. Law Review Vol.60 (1998) p. 149 at p. 155.

Fair use is a privilege in others than the owner of the copy right to use the copyrighted material in a reasonable manner without his consent.[353]

Fair use is available to the defendant as a defense when,(a) Market failure is present,(b) Transfer and (c) Ignorance Transfer of the use to the defendant is socially desirable and an award of the use to the defendant is socially desirable and an award of fair use would not cause substantial injury to the copyright owner.[354]

Several factors will play an important role in determining whether a given online use of a work is "fair work is "fair", infringing.

For the legal practitioner, the first important question in making judgments with respect to the assertion of a decencies whether the website operator is directly or indirectly involved in the allegedly infringing acts. There are at least two reasons why it is important to determine whether liability is direct or Indirect. First, if there is direct Infringement of any of the rights set forth in section 106 of the United Stated Copyright Act, then any defenses, particularly of fair use, would, if there is no possibility of the operator being directly liable, then the operator would have no copyright liability if the end user's is a fair one. This is because there can be no contributory or vicarious copyright liability without a finding that another

---

[353] Harper and Row 471 US at 549, if Maureen A.O. Rourke, Toward a Doctrine of Fair Use in Patent Law, Columbia Law Review Vol. 1000 (2000) p. 1177 at p. 1188.

[354] Wendy J.Gordon, Fair use as Market Failure: A structural and Economic Analysis of Betamax case and its Predecessors, Columbia Law Review Vol. 82 (1982) P. 1600.

person is directly liable.[355] The distinction between direct and indirect liability often forms the starting point of a fair use analysis in the online context. Once that threshold issue is determined, courts consider the traditional fair use factors as applied to various online activities. Importantly, several courts have rejected application of fair use defense to specific online activities by focusing on the effect of the conduct on potential marks for the copyrighted work.[356] Thus the court found that defendant copying of plaintiff's sound recordings and distribution of the recordings over the Internet infringed plaintiff's right to license those recordings, although plaintiff's were not engaged in such licensing[357]. Similarly, in Napster litigation, the court rejected the defendant's fair use argument with respect to the principal uses of the Napster service, because, in large part it credited the recording industry's studies showing that sales of compact disks suffered near college campuses where large number of Napster users reportedly dwelled.[358]

In another case, however, the court ruled that there was a triable issue of fact regarding an online service provider defendant's fair use defense, in particular as to lack of impairment of the potential market for the infringed works.[359] Indeed, the court stated that the defendant, Netcom on -line

---

[355] Cable/Home Communication Corp. v. Network Production, Inc., 902 F. 02 F.2d 829.

[356] Religious Technology Center v. Netcom Online Communication Services, 907 F.Supp. 1361.

[357] UMG Recordings Inc. v. MP3. Com, Inc. 92 F.Supp. 2d 349.

[358] A& M Records, Inc. v. Napster Inc., 54 U.S.P.Q 2d (BNA) 1746 N.D.California, 2000.

[359] Religious Technology Center v. Netcom Online Communication Services, 907 F.Supp. 1361, N.D.California, 1995.

communication service, easily might prevail on its fair use defence at trail. The court also held that the first two of the four fair use factors clearly cut in Netcom's favour. The purpose and character of Netcom's use weighed in its favour because, although commercial, Netcom's use also benefits the public in allowing for the functioning of the Internet and the dissemination of other creative works, which was considered to be the goal of the copyright Act[360]. Furthermore, because Netcom's revenue was based on fixed rates, and because there was no reasonably practical way for Netcom to obtain licenses for all works, the purpose and character of Netcom's use were not to obtain revenue and profit without paying the concomitant royalties.[361]

I case involving plaintiff's associated with the Church of Scientology, courts have held that the fair use doctrine protects both users online browsing of textual materials and the scanning or inputting of entire copies of works into a computer for purpose of private use and study[362]. Where, however a defendant copied entire news articles and posted them on a website for commentary, the court conclude that such actions were not excused by the fair use doctrine, because the entirely of articles was copied, the ability to post criticism was not "transformative", and the use, if permitted, would impair the plaintiff's ability to license their works.[363]

In case of copying by a search engine or other information locating functions, it was held in one case that when such

---

[360]   Ibid.

[361]   Religious Technology Center v. Netcom Online Communication Services, 907, F.Supp. 1361 N.D.California, 1995.

[362]   Ibid at 1378.

[363]   L.A. Times v. Free Republic, 54 USPQ 2d 1453.

a website copies a work in the course of presenting the information that it finds in response to a user's request, that copying is likely to be fair use.[364] The defendant's image search engine indexed plaintiff's photographer's website and displayed "thumbnails" of his works. The court found that defendant's use was a fair use because the thumbnail images were transformative and they were used for accessing information on the Internet, and not for the artistic expression they conveyed; the thumbnail images were small and had low resolution, and lost clarity when enlarged.[365] The court further noted that there was no market harm to plaintiff's sales and licensing of his photographs because the thumbnail images would not be a substitute for the full - sized images, and also because the search engine did not sell or license images' and actually directed traffic to the copyright owner's website[366]. By contrast, it might be noted that if the defendant were to have copied large and commercially significant portions of works verbatim, such use would not be transformative and would not likely excused as fair.[367]

United States Congress has set out in the copyright Act[368]. four non- excusive factors to be considered in determining whether the defense of fair use is appropriate. Firstly, the purpose and character of the use, including whether its use

---

[364] Kelly v. Arriba Soft Corporation, 77 F.Supp. 2d 1116 C.D. California. 1999.

[365] Ibid at 818-19.

[366] Ibid at 821-22.

[367] The Court in Kelly remanded to the District court the issue of whether displaying full-sized images of the copyrighted photographs would be infringing.

[368] United States Copyright Act, 976, Sec. 107.

is of a commercial or educational nature. That is the test to determine, if the purpose of the use was commercial or nonprofit educational methods. In a case[369], the United States Supreme Court stated that commercial use of copyright material raises a presumption of unfair use, that must be rebutted by the defendant.

Although nonprofit educational institutions that distribute copyright material are inclined to have benefit of fair use, they must be aware of its limitations. Courts have found copyright infringement for teachers distributing substantial photocopies of portions of books in class and the classroom and unauthorized videotaped material.[370] Likewise there are possibilities of online infringement. Second factor is the nature of the copyright material. Here courts will examine the nature of the work to determine if it is merely informational or factual. Newsworthy events and mere information are generally subject to fair use.

Third is the amount and substantiality of the copyright material in relation to the copyright work as a whole. This criterion is quantifiable and relates to the number of pages used. Distribution of a page or two may be appropriate, but a small critical portion may implicate infringement liability.[371] This limitation may be of special importance, if user in a nonprofit institution should download an entire program.

Fourth factor is the impact of the use on the potential market value of the copyright material. The courts will be

---

[369] Sony Corporation. V. Universal City studios, Inc., 464 U.S. 417 (1984).

[370] Marcus v. Rowley, 695 F. 2d 1171(9th cir. 1983).

[371] Harper & Row Publishers, Inc. v. Nation Enter; 471(U.S. 539, 1985).

unwilling to find fair use if the plaintiff can prove that due to the defendant's copying; the value occur either currently or potentially. Even with the first three criteria satisfied, there will not be fair use if the potential market of the copyright material is lost.[372]

The United State Supreme Court has stated, fair use when, properly applied, is limited to copying by others which does not materially impair the marketability of the work copied.[373]

Since Internet is seen as a source of information, the user rightly expects flow of information from the Internet. Then the user's right to information or freedom of information should also have to given consideration. In India right to information is recognized as a fundamental right flowing from Article 19(1)(2) of the Indian Constitution[374]. Therefore it can be considered as a public interest, which is against the author's right. Fair Use Doctrine could be the obvious solution to this problem.

First Sale Doctrine

The first sale doctrine[375] limits the copyright owner's exclusive right to distribute publicly a copy of the work when the copyright material was lawfully required by another.

---

[372] American Geophysical Union v. Texaco, Inc. 37 F. 3d 881 2nd Cir.(1994).

[373] Harper & Row Publishers, Inc. v. Nation Enter; 471 (U.S. 539, 1985).

[374] Dr. A. David Ambrose, Judicial Response to Right to Information in India Delhi Law Review vol. XXI (1999) pp. 70-82.

[375] United States Copyright Act, 1976, Sec. 109(a)

Under the Copyright Act, "The owner of a copy.............. Is entitled, without the authority of the copyright owner, to sell........ that copy"[376]. This probably will help to sell this text book, and can do so without violating its copyright. Consider the case of a text book purchase in electronic from, transferred and delivered to a student through the internet. If it is resold electronically, it would involve the infringing acts of reproduction and public display of the text book that are not permitted under the first sale doctrine. The first person who owned the book also retained a copy, so the first sale doctrine does not permit the distribution of a copy through the Internet.[377]

Public domain

Materials in public domain are not subject to the exclusive statutory rights of copyright owner. There is a concept that everything in Internet is in public domain and id freely available to the public. But it is not an accepted theory.

Remedies for Infringement

The copyright holders have a duty to be more diligent to protect their rights through both Civil[378] and Criminal remedies[379]. While civil remedies compensate the owner, the criminal remedies act as a deterrent against infringing

---

[376] Ibid. Sec. 19

[377] Ferrera, Lichtenstein, Reder, Bird, Sachiano: Cyberlaw –Text & Cases, 2nd Ed. 2003, Thomson, South – Western West. P.99.

[378] Indian Copyright Act, 1957, Ch XII

[379] Ibid, Ch XIII.

activities. But to sustain a criminal proceeding under the Act, the knowledge of the infringing party to infringe the rights shall be proved beyond doubt.

Civil Remedies

Copyright is a property right, and where infringement has been proved, the copyright owner can, subject to certain special rules, benefit from 'all such relief …………. As is available in respect of the infringement of any other property right[380]. In practice the principal remedies are injunctions to prevent further breaches of copyright, damages for breach of copyright and order for delivery up of infringing copies. Other remedies include accounts of profits and order for disposal of infringing copies which have been seized or delivered up to a claimant.[381]

Various court orders can be obtained at the pre- trail stage, in some circumstances without the alleged infringes being given any warning or opportunity to make representations to the court. One such order that has been used is the 'search order'[382]. Such an order can authorize a claimant to enter a defendant's premises, without prior warning, to seize evidentiary material which might otherwise be tempered with disappear before trial.

This is obviously a powerful remedy capable of abuse in the hands of overenthusiastic claimants and the courts now

---

[380] CDPA, 1988, Sec.96

[381] Ibid, Sec. 96-106 and 113-115.

[382] Formally called an 'Anton Piller order' after the case in which it was first obtained. Anton piller KG v. Manufacturing process Ltd. (1976) Ch.55.; Gates v. Swift (1981) FSR 57.

supervise its use quite strictly.[383] While final injunction may be prohibitory, enjoining a defendant from copying or in any way dealing with the material that is the subject of the dispute.[384] Alternatively, or in addition, an injunction may be mandatory.[385]

As a general rule, damages for copyright infringement are intended to compensate a claimant for actual loss incurred as a result of the infringement. This might typically be calculated on the basis of royalties which have been payable to the claimant by the defendant, instead of infringing copyright, obtained a licence for the question.

Criminal remedies

With an intention to penalize those who deliberately infringe copyright with a view to commercial gain, the Copyright Act has set out a number of categories of criminal copyright infringement[386]. Any person who knowingly infringes or abets the infringement of copyright or any other right envisaged by the Act shall be liable to be punished with imprisonment which may vary between six months to three years or a fine ranging from Rs.50000/- to Rs. Two lakhs. But if the infringement is not made for gain in the course of trade or business, a lesser sentence is permitted[387].Only a person who

---

[383]   Systematic Ltd. v. London Computer Center Ltd. (1983) FSR 313.

[384]   Raindrop Data Systems Ltd. v. Systematics Ltd. (1988) FSR. 354.

[385]   Redwood Music Ltd. v. Chappel & Co. Ltd (1982) RPC 109.

[386]   CDPA, 1988

[387]   Indian Copyright Act, 1957, Sec.63.

knowingly infringes or abets the infringement, falls within the purview of the section. Mere possibility of this having been known would not suffice. There has to be clear and conclusive proof of the requisite knowledge and the existence of reasonable means of knowing is not enough.[388]

As part of DMCA, the United States Online Copyright Infringement Liability Limitation Act was enacted, which adds a new section 512,[389] which is dealing with the enforcement of copyrights. The DMCA creates civil remedies and criminal penalties. A civil action may be brought in a federal district court.[390] The court may also order the impounding, the remedial modification or the destruction of the devices or products involved in the violation. The court has broad powers to grant injunctions and award damages, costs and attorney's fees[391]. The court may punish repeat offenders by awarding treble damage awards[392] against innocent violators. But, in the case of nonprofit library, archives, educational institutions, the court must remit damages, if it finds that a qualifying entity had no reason to know of the violation.[393] The DMCA prescribes significant criminal penalties foe willful violation committed for commercial advantage or private financial gain.[394] Criminal penalties are inapplicable to nonprofit libraries, archives, and educational institutions.[395]

---

[388] A.K. Mukerjee v. State (1994) 54 DLT 461.
[389] United States Copyright Act 1976, Ch.5.
[390] DMCA, 1998, Sec. 1203 (a)
[391] Ibid, Sec.1203 (b)
[392] Ibid, Sec. 1203 (c)(4)
[393] Ibid, Sec. 1203 (c)(5)
[394] DMCA 1998, Sec. 1204 (a)
[395] Ibid, Sec. 1204 (b).

Jurisdiction

One of the major issue dealing with copyright in cyberspace is Jurisdiction[396]. Until now, copyright has been protected by national legislation confined within the territorial boards of states. International protection is granted through the implementation of International Treaties.[397] Basically the aim of these treaties is the synchronization of different territorial laws on copyright to lessen inconsistency in protection, by laying down some minimum standards. On the other hand, cyberspace has no geographical boundaries. There is no specific case law to point on Internet Jurisdiction. The approach from U.K. and United State is that which suggest a movement away from holding that, simply because a site can be accused from a given territory, that territory should have Jurisdiction over the Internet. However one should be cautious and not jump to conclusions from such limited case law.[398]

Information Technology Act, 2000

Information Technology Act provides for civil and criminal consequence. The Act prescribes penalty against a person who without permission of the owner accesses, or download s or

---

[396] Joana Zakalik, International Jurisdiction and conflict of Law in Cyberspace http://www.libraries. Wayne:edu/-/joltman/ pzakalik.html/ visited on 02.02.2007.

[397] Berne convention, Universal copyright convention, WIPO Treaties and lastly TRIPS.

[398] Alan, Williams, Duncan Calow, Nickhigham, Digital Media-Contracts, Right and Licensing, Sweet and Maxwell, 2nd Ed., 1998, p. 399-400.

introduces virus or causes may damage, or disrupts, or denies access to an authorized person to any computer, computer system or computer network or charges service to the account of any other person. The penalty can be extended to one crore rupees[399]. Chapter x1 of the Information Technology Act deals with criminal liability.[400]

A major issue to be dealt by the copyright lawyers at the present time is how to deal with the arrival and rapid development of the Internet. The worldwide telecommunication system permits rapid and instantaneous transmission around the world. It included entertainments in all media print, picture, stills and movies, sounds, combinations, etc[401]. Thus the Internet presents new problems to the copyright law. There is no reason to doubt the copyright law that, it cannot be adopted to deal with them.[402]

When seeking a remedy for Internet copyright Infringement, it is difficult to assess the unwarranted laws. The copyright laws, even though they try to be more compliant, are not constituted in the light of the digital environment. When looking for a reasonable approach to copyright liability of Internet, the interest of content and service providers, of users and of authors have to be taken into account. The interest of having full access to all Information has to be weighed against the need for the author's protection.

The Indian Jurisprudence in the area of Internet related offences is still in its starting stage and there is not so much case

---

[399] Information Technology Act 2000, Sec. 43.
[400] Ibid, Ss. 65 and 66
[401] Hector L. Macqueen, Copyright and the Internet 98 CLR 647.
[402] Ibid.

laws on this subject. But in one case[403], the plaintiff's made a herbal database and posted on it's website. An Italian company copied it through a United State sever. Indian company filed a suit in the High Court of Delhi which granted an ex parte injunction in the favour of the Indian company and a notice was served to the defendant, thus removed the database from the website.

Digital haves and -notes may create by the widespread move towards the online delivery of works on any form of fee - for access basis.[404] Even the 2008 Amendment Act not proposed any particular change in this regard.

---

403 Himalayan Drugs Company v. Sumit.

404 Robert Burrell and Allison Coleman, Copyright Exceptions. The Digital ImpAct, Cambridge studies in Intellectual Property Rights, Sweet & Maxwell. 2005, p.77.

CHAPTER VI

Internet and Moral Rights

Everyone has the right to the protection of moral and material interests resulting from any scientific, literary or Artistic production of which he is the author.[405]

The copyright besides conferring economic rights also confers moral rights to the author. Moral rights are the rights that related to the honour and integrity of the creator of the works. It is more personal than economic right.

Moral rights grew up in continental Europe during the 19th century and find their philosophical justification in the idea that an author's work is an extension of his personality and any assault on the woek is as much an attack on the author as a physical assault.

---

[405] UDHR, Art. 27(2)

With in Common Law, moral rights are regarded, not as a nebulous manifestation of relationship, but as a bundle of relatively rigid, distinct and somewhat disconnected rights.[406]

France is normally held up as the model for moral rights law, by relying on general tortuous liability under their Civil Code.[407] The moral rights are considered as an incorporeal property where the author's rights are separable into patrimonial rights and moral rights as held by the Dualist[408]. The Monists[409] considered the moral rights as exploitative interests to from a single rights.[410] Moral rights having a considerable focus of interest in the discussions of Berne Convention[411] which lead to the adoption of Berne Convention Implementation Act of 1988 in U.S which recognizes some of the rights and required its member states to provide the author with the right to claim authorship and to object to any alterations, distortions or mutilation of, or other derogatory action in relation to the said work, which would be prejudicial to his honour or reputation.

---

[406] Frederic Polloud, The Internet and Author's Rights, Perspective on Intellectual Property. Vole 5, Sweet and Maxwell, London. 1999, p. 89-102.

[407] French Civil Code, Art. 1382

[408] Mainly the French Scholars

[409] The Germans

[410] J.S. Stromhom, I Droit Moral de L'Auteur, 1966, p. 150-53.

[411] Berne Convention, 1928, Art. 6 bis.

Countries like U.S,[412] U.K,[413] South Africa[414], New Zealand[415] and Australia[416] etc. have full specific statutory protection regarding the moral rights.

Justification to Protect Moral Rights in Internet

The primary justification for the protection of moral right is the idea that the work of art is an extension of the artist's personality[417], an expression of his innermost being. To mistreat the work of art is to mistreat the artist, to invade his area of privacy and impair his personality.

The Internet presents enormous opportunities for artistic and literary creation and recreation. The ease of transmission from creator to viewer, and on from viewer to viewer, makes the Internet an ideal medium for artists and author's to disseminate their works. Simultaneously technology provides the potential for any of these viewers to quickly and easily edit, alter, distort or redistribute an original works without the author's permission.[418]

The belief behind moral right is that, even though it is extended to digital media, the authors are almighty creators who pour particular meaning into their creation and therefore inherently have disputed authority over the uses and

---

[412] Berne Convention Implementation Act, 1988 (BCIA), U.S
[413] CDPA, 1988, Ss. 77-89
[414] South African Copyright Act, 1988, Ss. 77-89
[415] New Zealand Copyright Act, 1978, Sec. 20
[416] Australian Copyright Amendment (Moral Rights) Act, 2002
[417] Natural Law Theory
[418] Yee Fen Lim, Cyberspace Law – Commentaries and Materials, Oxford Universities Press, 2002, p. 382

interpretation of these creations.[419] Thus the author projects part of his personality into the world and subjects it for public use. Therefore an author, even in cyberspace, needs protection from a savage public use.[420] An author has, in a sense made a gift to the society in respect of his creative genius.[421] So the purpose of moral right is to recognize and encourage the result of intellectual creativity on a level with other forms of property. In the Internet, it is more easy to destruct an authors moral rights because of the technological advancement and so appropriate moral right protection should have to extend to the Internet also.

More over, parting with the copyright does not lessen the author's personal attachment to the works. It follows that the author should have recourse against those who present the work differently from the away the author originally intended. This theory include right such as the right to decide when to first publish to prevent excessive criticism of the work, and even to withdraw a work from circulation when it no longer represent's the author's views.[422]

---

[419] Beyer, Internationalism, Art and the suppression of Innovation: Film Colorization and the Philosophy of Moral Rights 82 NW Rev. 1011, 1027 (1988).

[420] Martin Roder, Doctrine of Moral Rights: A Study in the Law of Artists, Authors and Creators 557(1940)

[421] Russel Dasilva, Droit Moral and the Amoral Copyright 28 (1980).

[422] D. Vaver, Moral Rights Yesterday, Today and Tomorrow, International Journal of Law and Information Technology, 7 (3), 2002, p. 270.

Forms of Moral Rights in Internet

Moral rights protection in relation to works in Internet has been a highly disputed issue. To what extent are multimedia works by their nature, a threat to their author's moral rights is a question which shall be resolved through certain regulations in this regard. Moral rights are to be personal to the author or creator of a work and are to be capable of exercise independently of the economic right[423] in the work.

There are numerous ways to misappropriate a creation on the Internet. It is possible to

a) Copy a work without permission or license.

b) Present the work as the works of oneself.

c) Produce an online parody or an online endorsement.

d) Reproduce the style of original creation, deliberately leading others to believe that the work is that of the original creator.

e) Fail to give credit for reproduction creator.

f) Inaccurately attribute credit in the case of a distributed works etc....[424]

The problems inherent in protecting moral rights and copyright are not exclusive to the Internet. What is exclusive to the Internet is the ease with which an author's work can be compromised.[425] Historically, to reproduce a work on a large scale required considerable investment of both time and

---

[423] Indian Copyright Act, 1957, Sec. 14.

[424] Yee Fen Lim, Cyberspace Law-Commentaries and Materials, Oxford University Press, 2002, p. 382.

[425] Ibid, p. 383.

money. With the advent of computer and later on the Internet, the obstacles to reproduction have, been considerably eroded. An individual who happens across a work, then decides to alter or misappropriate it, might contravene both the moral rights of the author and the copyright of the copyright holder.

Moral right is thus inalienable from the author and is available even after the transfer of this economic rights as held by Delhi High Court in one case[426] in which the defendant is restraining from the infringement action on the ground of distortion and mutilation.

The moral rights are generally accepted into, right of paternity, right of integrity, right of disclosure and right against false attribution. In the context of Internet also all these right can be attributed, remain with the authors and last through out the entire term of copyright. Some of the moral rights are recognized as "Author's special rights"[427] in India, they are right to claim authorship of the work and the right or restoration or claim damages.[428]

Right to Paternity and Internet

The right of paternity safeguards creators right to have his name attached to the work or to claim authorship of the work.[429] Generally this rights perpetually un assignable and is not barred by statutes of limitation. Moreover the rights of paternity protects against falsely attaching mode of

---

[426] Manu Bhandari v. Kala Vikas Pictures, AIR 1987 Del. 13.

[427] Indian Copyright Act, 1957 (1994 Amendment), Sec. 57

[428] Manu Bhandari v. Kala Vikas Pictures, AIR 1987, Del., 13.

[429] Jack. A. Clive, Moral Rights: The long and Winding Road Toward Recognition, 1990, p. 435.

identification can be used by the author, but it must be clear and prominent. In the case of commercial exploitation of the work, the author should be identified in each copy.

The right of paternity is more important in the digital context because any unauthorized alteration is easily possible in Internet, which may badly affect the authorship of a work. The author of a work in Internet will not be, entitled to the right of paternity, if he is not asserted it or if he has waited it or if he an employee of the producer of the work.[430] In U.K. it is 'to be identified as such[431]. The right of paternity must be asserted in writing and in most cases only bind third paternity must be asserted in writing and in most cases only bind parties who have notice of it[432]. In the case of works created in the course of employment, the right does not apply to anything done by, or with the authority of, the employer or any subsequent owner of a copyright in the work.[433]

In fact the author of a work in internet should have his work attributed to him. This has a twofold importance in a digital context. Firstly, it represents one of the essential human right based rights, that should be represents one of the essential human right based rights, that should be granted to any author of a copyrighted work as part of his personality. Secondly, in a digital environment, where pirated material is difficult to distinguish from original materials. The right of paternity helps to assure the public that what it received on its screen is

---

430 Irini A Stamatoudi, Copyright and Multimedia Works, 1st Ed., Cambridge University Press, p. 228.

431 CDPA 1988, Sec. 77

432 Ibid, Sec. 78

433 Ibid, Sec. 79(3)

the original work and not copies that have been tempered[434]. Such a right should be absolute. It should not be subject to additional requirements or formalities such as assertion and it should also not be waivable.

Right of Integrity and Internet

The right of integrity[435] is also known as the right to object derogatory treatment. This right prohibits the modification, alteration or distortion of any work without the author's permission[436]. The right of integrity just as the tight of paternity is generally perpetual, un assignable and free from any status of limitation.

In the digital media also, as in the case of analogue media, authors have the right to object derogatory treatment of their works[437]. Treatment of a work will be deemed derogatory if it amounts to distortion or mutilation of the work or is otherwise prejudicial to the honour or reputation of the author.[438]

The interactive capability of the work which the public can access on -line and the technical skill of some copyright offenders, facilitates even more the alteration, distortion, destruction or removal of their content, actions etc. which obviously threaten the essence of the principles of this moral

---

[434] Yee Fen Lim, Cyberspace Law-Commentaries and Materials, Oxford University Press, 2002, p. 382.

[435] The right to prevent alteration and other action that may damage the author's honour or reputation.

[436] Berne Convention, Art. 6 bis.

[437] CDPA, 1988, Sec. 80(1)

[438] Ibid, Sec. 80(2)

right.[439] Thus the intended use and reinforcement of the right of integrity in Internet is two conflicting views which should have given immediate concern.

The claims of moral rights and its enforcement is either unjustified or far reaching. If one wants to restrict, the right of integrity and right of paternity from being infringed, only if there is damage to the authors honour and reputation. This view is based on Anglo -Saxon presumption that a distortion or mutilation does not necessarily prejudice the authors honour and reputation. Such a requirement army fall within the scope of formal use of a multimedia work, which clearly allow the change of the work. But it gives away a substantial part of the author's integrity right without his consent and should be rejected on the ground that, although not affecting the author honour and reputation, does nevertheless affect the right and original form of the work.

In case of more creative work, the right of integrity should be applied more strictly. This proposition must prove to be very important in relation to multimedia products and their multifarious nature. Yet the proposition applies any litigation process and a case by case basis. The Belgium and Germen copyright law an overall moral rights for the future is void.[440] Moral rights can be waived in specific cases that are strictly defined in relation to existing works only. Moreover, any of the moral rights 'may be viewed by instrument in writing signed by the person giving up the right'. Such waivers may relate to specific works or to works generally, may be conditional or

---

[439]   Julian Rodriguez Pardo, Copyright and Multimedia, Kulwer Law International, 2003. P. 75

[440]   Belgium Copyright Act 1994, Art. 1(2)(2)

unconditional, and may be made subject to revocation[441]. But under French Law, Waivers of moral rights are not possible.[442]

Remedies For Breach of Moral Rights

An infringement of moral rights is actionable as breach of statutory duty owed to a person entitled to the right[443]. Mandatory injunction will be relevant, where judge orders that the author's name is added in copies of the remaining works and to future copies. Moreover an injunction may be appropriate to prevent the planned publications of or broadcast of a derogatory treatment of the woks.[444]

Usually damages are available for the breach of a statutory duty and in the case of infringement of the moral rights, this would appear to include damages for non- economic loss. In fact the moral rights are non- economic in nature. Additional damages are available[445]. However in a case which indicates that damages for false attribution may be slight in comparison with those available for defamation[446].Moreover the court has a discretion in a case involving the alleged infringement of the right to object to derogatory treatment conditionally to grant prohibitory injunction requiring that dissociating the author

---

[441] CDPA, 1988, Sec. 87

[442] In French, infringement of droit moral is usually regarded as raising questions of honour, which are remedial by judicial recognition of that infringement.

[443] CDPA, 1988, Sec. 103(1)

[444] Bainbridge: Intellectual Property Law, 4th Ed. Financial Time Pitman Publications, 1999, p. 118.

[445] CDPA, 1988, Sec. 97(2).

[446] Moore v. Daily News Plc. 1972, 1, A.B, 441

from the treatment of the work.[447] In relation to the right of paternity, the court must take into account any delay in asserting the right.[448] Both of these qualifications on remedies have the effect of further limiting the potential commercial leverage which moral rights may confer on an author.

Indian Court has taken affirmative decisions in a series of cases in relation to moral rights. The moral right remain with the author and are enforceable, even if all the economic rights have been assigned or licensed[449]. It was further affirmed by a case[450] that the moral rights thus provide the rights to assert the authorship of a work and also right of integrity. The court in another case[451] held that the plaintiff was entitled to an injunction restraining the defendant from further deterioration of the plaintiff's works, which would be prejudicial to the plaintiff's honour and reputation. Thus the Indian Courts put the moral rights on a higher grade than the normal object of copyright.[452] The language of the provision containing special rights is of widest amplitude. It cannot be restricted to literary expression only. Visual and audio - manifestations are also

---

[447] CDPA, 1988, Sec. 103(2)

[448] Ibid, Sec. 78(5)

[449] K.P.M. Sundaram v. Ratton Prakashan Mandir and Other, AIR, 1983, Del. 461

[450] Wilay Eastern Ltd. v. Indian Institute of Management, 58 (1995), DLT, 449

[451] Amar Nath Sengal v. Union of India, 2002, (25) PTC, C-56, Delhi

[452] Indian Copyright Act, 1957, Sec. 57

directly covered[453]. This section lifts the authors status above the material gain of copyright and gives him a special position.

Since these are inalienable and un transferable rights that cannot be waived-[454] the moral rights of the other of a work in Internet are not different from those enjoyed by other author of moral conversational works, since their content cannot be arbitrarily recognized according to the person to whom they belong. Therefore based on Berne Convention[455], the author of a work in Internet is basically entitled to two moral rights, that is the right of paternity and the right of integrity, because of the reason that in this digital era, distortion and alteration of the work is very easy.

Ultimately, the solution to the problem army be technical, just as the concept of automatic electronic billing is being developed to allow legitimate uses in relation to protected economic rights. So the advent of digital "water marking"[456] of files will enable easier taking of copies, even those that are partial or transformed, for the purpose of asserting the rights of paternity and integrity.[457]

---

[453] Justice A.S. Strivastava, Lal's Commentary on the Copyright Act, 3rd Ed., Delhi law House, 2004, p. 659

[454] UDHR, Art. 27

[455] Berne Convention, Art. 6 bis.

[456] A process of encoding information about the origin and contents of a file as a part of the file itself.

[457] Frederic Polloud-Dulian; The Internet and Author's Rights; Perspective on Intellectual Property, Vol.5, Sweet & Maxwell, London, 1999, p. 100.

CONCLUSIONS

The analysis of the study brings into view two important aspects, that the Internet as a medium is to stay and that it has be taken seriously and that the exiting Intellectual property regime fails when it comes to dealing with the protection of the right of author's in Internet.

The issue that arises is whether one wants to extend the existing Intellectual property Regime to the Internet or else let the Internet find solutions for itself, or else should there be new system of law that would possibly govern the copyright protection on the Internet.

It does not make any sense to have a new or a sui generic system of law that would take care of this problem. While we take In to consideration about the idea that the Internet can given itself and take care of the problems that it faces is appealing, one has take into account the quantum of infringement that is being done on the Internet. This aspect cannot be ignored and in order to facilitate and protect the interest of the authors, it army be possible to have some law in a form that would deal with the issues of copyright protection on the Internet.

The question, then, is whether to enact a whole new system of laws that deal with the copyright protection on the Internet or Think twice before modifying the existing regime. In this twenty -first century, which is witnessing a battle of fundamentals between two opposite view of online world, that is freedom of information and right to protection of copyright owner's legitimate interest. The legislature and the court should have to look into this aspect seriously.

By considering various issues related to other's right in the digital world, the main focus is on the enforcement mechanism and the jurisdiction aspects. From this brief analysis the important point is that, the role of the legislature especially in the Indian context, where, w e still don't have an apt legal frame work for the protection of this current issues, which still is an emerging concept, w hen compared with the western countries. They have at least a systematic approach towards such protection without such a framework, a piracy in the Internet is very easy. Therefore it is the duty of the legislature to sub serve the changing needs of the society and technology.

There is a viewed that the present copyright law is enough to sub serve the modern technological changes through proper interpretation. But there is no need to say that the vast interpretations can introduce ambiguity in the law. So clear cut provisions are very much necessary.

In the Indian Copyright Act, there is an exception for infringement when it is comes to the point of fair use. Fair use includes research for private study, criticism, review etc., which are mainly academic in nature. The spirit of the legislature in making this law was promote academic as well as research interests., but now it has become a very large loophole. This tendency show the weakness of the present law. We need strong national laws to curb the weakness of the present law. We need strong national laws to curb the cyber piracy. Thus Digital Millennium Copyright Act is a very good example for this and it is their quick response towards the changing trends of the society. Our legal system is yet to be equipped and we should have digital copyright legislation to cope up with the technology. Regarding the Internet, When related to the copyright, we have potentially no low to protect them. This lawlessness leads towards a huge loss of Intellectual property of the cyberspace. It is also providers a very good soil for new spurts in cyber piracy.

By the new introduction of the uniformity of applications to state laws internationally, the international organizations have got a great role in curbing the digital piracy. It is true that every state should have its own anti- piracy laws. But due to the international nature of the cyber space, we need some controlling and unifying agreements internationally. The state laws may not be always reciprocal to each other and they are formed to sub serve the needs of a particular state. Now we can take the rational idea behind the Berne conventions and the WIPO copyright conventions, all of which deals with International Intellectual Property Rights regarding copyright protection. But the problem is that, they are not in harmonizing nature, which again creates confusion. The Indian Information Technology Act, 2000 is an example for the national law, which is aided by the UNCITRAL Model Law. Likewise to protect cyber Intellectual property, there can be a global law, which aids the national law with the help of international organizations. Thus, the model law can solve the technical problems of time, jurisdiction etc.. In this manner, in the relevant law, the severity of the punishment for infringement and jurisdiction can clearly be decided according to the necessity.

Moreover, awareness programmes is an important concern. The people are to be given an awareness of copyright protection on the Internet. To a certain extent, such efforts help to control the cyber piracy. The public also is expected to have a role, perhaps, the most important one. They can be made aware of the copyright laws which helps them to be very familiar with the violation of the laws concerned in the digital age. This will help to reduce the copying of unauthorized article from the Internet. The cautious approach to cyber intellectual property rights is also very important. Another important role of public is in their reporting the violation of the rules to the appropriate authority. These efforts thus will heighten public awareness of the dangers of caching and pop up advertising, which has become a nuisance to the users f of the Internet. Internet piracy is being done in order to defraud or deceive the public for monetary gain.

Another newly emerging self -mechanism is the DRM, that is Digital Rights Management, which protects the digital Intellectual Property Rights. At present, it is widely experimented in digital music area and the next wave is predicted to be 'e -books'. soft -ware vendors and video game companies are also expected to need and use DRM sooner. DRM helps to protect content on the net, usually by encrypting it. The key to decryption is given to genuine license holders. DRM also has certain "authoring rights" but into it, depending on what the content creator wants to offer customers. DRM, by its peculiar nature, can work as a sample service to customers. It seems to be very much helpful to protect the digital rights of copyright owner. However, the reporting is always very much important even after the company faces violations, using the DRM mechanism. The widespread and growing use of technology for the transfer and dissemination of information and services to ever- wider audience is a great challenge to the law and the society. The joint efforts of the machineries of the government through legislations, administrations and proper interpretation are very much important to control the cyber medium. Other than cyber policing, the method of self - policing that the individuals and companies can follow should be adopted. Therefore the concept of Digital Rights Management is another effective measure to control cyber piracy.

In the recent years, India has come to be known as an international community as an information technology major. The development and growth of online means of transmission of copyrighted works over the Internet has thrown up a surplus of issue of immediate relevance and therefore there is a compelling need for India to conform to the International framework for resolution of these issues. There are, however, issues of relevance that the current legal framework does not provide for any statutory remedies such as liabilities and activities of intermediaries for copyright infringement, the rights management information, and the protection of anti-circumvention devices etc. ...Hence barring a few important aspects, India's copyright laws does not meet the challenges posted by the Internet.

The Intellectual property is the wealth of nations. The misappropriation and destruction of this property can imbalance the economic infrastructure of the nation. When it comes to the Intellectual property of cyberspace, especially Internet, it is very much vulnerable to appropriation as, it would cheaply be reproduced. However, in this global village, for the time being, we cannot expect a copyright protected digital environment. But infallible legislations with proper punishments, efficient technological mechanism and enlightened netizens can together create a peaceful net environment in this cyber age.

By addressing all these issues, one will have to be very clear as regards what stands one wants to take and in implementing it but we have to see that all people's interest are properly well balanced.

TEACH ACT

In United States, the Technology, Education and Copyright Harmonization Act generally called as TEACH Act attempts to improve upon some of the restrictive nature of the DMCA by offering many improvements over the previous version of section 110(2) of copyright legislation in addition, this Act updates copyright law in the area of digital online education and, if the requirements are met, facilitates the use of copyrighted materials in digital online education efforts without having to obtain prior permission from the copyright owner. TEACH Act make five basic changes to previous copyright legislation.

a) "It expands the categories of works that can be performed in distance education beyond non dramatic literary and musical works to reasonable and limited portions of other works, with the exception of works produced primarily for the education market.

b) It removes the concept of the physical classroom and recognizes that a student should be able to access the digital content of a course where he or she has access to a computer.

c) It allows storage of copyrighted materials on a server to permit asynchronous performances and displays.

d) It permits institutions to digitize works to use in distance education when digital version do not already exist and when the digital work is not subject to protection measures that prevent its use.

e) It clarifies that participants in authorized distance education courses and programs are not liable for infringement for any transient or temporary reproductions that occurs through the automatic technical process of digital transmission"[458]

Fair use exception in India can be extended along with this line for adequate and effective online education.

A critical Analysis of Indian Copyright Act

In the Internet, the problems due to uploading and downloading can be solved by providing guidelines regarding the type of materials allowable on a site. Moreover the liability for the violation of such guidelines should be posted explicitly on the website. Precise Police for removing possible infringing of contents should provided.

To prevent others to link their sites, copyright owners should arrange their technological and legal fences[459]. In case framing also such technological and legal fences along

---

[458] I.N. Gasaway, (2001, November), Balancing Copyright Concerns: The TEACH Act of 2001 EDUCAUSE Review 36(6) 82-83.

[459] Ejaan Maakay, The Economics of Emerging Property Rights on the Internet, The Future of copyright in a Digital Environment, P. Bernt Hughenolotz Ed. 1996, p. 25.

with contracts through which framing can be disallowed and enabling the user to see entire framed page. Effectively controlling access to a work is strictly a technological measure which can apply with the authority of the copyright owner to gain access to the work. It can be considered as an act of circumvention.[460] Linking, framing etc.... Should only be permitted upon license or permission from the copyright holder, which attracts a future development of internet as a market place.[461] In case of caching there are three alternative solutions, like:-

   a)   Collective Licensing
   b)   Technical solutions
   c)   Code of conduct.

Collective Licensing is proved as a viable solution even in cases of large, loosely organized user groups. For this purpose, right organizations should encourage various types of multimedia licensing that would involve co-operation between different categories of right holders. This would enable the granting of wide range of rights for electronic uses.

In case of technical solutions, the copyright holders is entitled to specify or control caching through technological means. It is practically possible, to create dynamic pages on website that are displayed to user only after the user initiates a server resident programme called by the name a Common Gateway Interface Script. This CGI script can be taken as a a

460   ECD, 2001, Art. 6.
461   Reno. V. ACLU, 117 S.C. 1239, 1997.

standard for interfacing external application with information servers. It permits the passing of information to particular user or classes of users. Using this mechanism, each subsequent request to file server for the same destination information specified by URL an return different information.

As far as codes of conduct is considered, parties concerned should draft jointly practicable and stable codes of codes of conduct, which serve as model for a legislative solution.

Moreover other challenges in Internet like pop-up advertising, Digital audio transmission etc... Should also be regulated by adopting such technical and other possible measures to protect the interest of the copyrights holder.

There is a need to amend the Indian Copyright Act, according to the changing scenario. To adjust with the digital media, an overall change from the definition itself is necessary.

The reproduction right of literary, dramatic or musical work, after the 1994 amendment include strong of it any medium by electronic means"[462]. The new definitions of cinematographic film[463] and sound recording[464] recognize it in any medium. That will include digital medium also.

---

[462] Indian Copyright (Amendment)Act 1994, Sec. 14(a)(1)
[463] Indian Copyright Act, 1957, Sec. 2(f)
[464] Ibid, Sec. 2(xx)

The right of communication to the public[465] is also available under the new definition in the context of digital technology as mentioned in WCT, ECD and DMCA. Thus, the right of communication recognize the making available of the work regardless of whether any member of the public actually sees or hears or otherwise enjoys the work so made available.[466] Therefore the authors of all categories of work is entitled to protect the online communication to the work. Even though the reproduction right and communication to the public right are extended to all types of works in the digital media, the Indian Copyright Act does not address storage of a work as it is a matter of interpretation to determine whether temporary and permanent reproduction will from part of this right. The U.S. Act[467] and E.C.D[468] clearly dealt with the above provisions to effectively protect and enforce the rights of copyright holder.

The distinctive characteristics of online dissemination of copyrighted work enhances the economic value of the copyright work. The Copyright Act confers the right to transfer of the copyrighted works[469] for this purpose. But this provision does not extend to the online dissemination of works. Thus unless a license to agreement expressly provides, courts should not extend the license to online distribution of a work. U.S and ECD also keep silence on this point.

---

[465]   Ibid, Sec. 2(ff)

[466]   Ibid, Sec. 14.

[467]   U.S. Copyright Act, 1976, Sec. 106

[468]   E.C.D, 2001, Art. 2.

[469]   Indian Copyright Act, 1957, Sec. 30.

To constitute infringement, it is necessary that a substantial, or material part of the work should be copied[470]. But there is no objective test to determine what is substantial. Substantiality is a question of fact and degree.[471] In the Internet also there is no such criteria to determine what constitute infringement. Here also DMCA and ECD is silent but in Singapore Copyright Amendment Act[472], there is a provision called reasonable portion, which means, in case of a stored on any medium by electronic means not more than 10 percent of the total number of bytes in that edition of the work is divided into chapters, not less than 10 percent of the total number of bytes in that edition. Similar provisions can be incorporated into the Indian copyright Act.

Moreover, regarding the theories of liability, Indian Act only mentioned about direct[473] and indirect infringement[474]. But keeping silence on contributory[475] and vicarious infringements[476], which is necessary in this online context for adequate and additional protection of the interests of the authors.

When taking the issue of jurisdiction, India is territorially bounded like U.K, U.S and European Union. Contrastingly,

---

[470] R.G. Anand v. Deluxe Films, AIR 1978, S.C, 1613.

[471] Wham-O-Manufacturing company v. Lincoln Industries, 1982, RPC 281.

[472] Singapore Copyright Amendment Act, 1999, Sec. 7(A)(2).

[473] Shyam Shah v. Gaya Prasad Guptha, AIR 1971, AII 192.

[474] Manfstaengal v. Empire Palace, (1894) 3ch. 109 & 127

[475] Sega Enterprises v. MAPHIA, 948 F.Supp. 679, N.D.California 1996.

[476] RIAA v. Napster, 114 F.Supp. 2d. 896, N.D.California, 2000.

digital environment is transnationally bounded. Therefore, when infringements are occurring in more than one place through digital media, which territory will apply and which law will prevail is still an unsolved issue. So we can find out a reasonable solution among the principles like country of protection, principle of origin and combined theory. Even though copyright protection varies from one country to another.

Though a copyright holder is entitled to certain civil[477] and criminal[478] remedies, it is not sufficient in the digital environment. So we can adopt the DMCA provisions regarding the civil[479] and criminal[480] remedies.

Moreover there are certain exceptions in case of infringement of copyright.[481] Even if this provision covers computer programmes, there is no express provisions relating to exceptions of infringement in Internet. It will not be possible for a user to access a website without technically infringing copyright of the website owner because once a user start surfing of a website, images may automatically stored in his computer. To take advantage of digital technologies, DMCA provides exemption for Library and Archives.[482] There is no exemption for ephemeral recording in Indian copyright Act fair dealing with respect to digital broadcast, but the same

---

477   Indian Copyright Act, 1957, ch. XII
478   Ibid, ch. XII
479   DMCA, 1998, Sec. 1203.
480   Ibid, Sec. 1204
481   Indian Copyright Act, 1957, Sec. 52.
482   DMCA, 1998, Sec. 404.

is precisely defined in DMCA[483]. Because of the lack of circumvention of technological measures, creative works are in - numerously pirated. Thus the copyright holders in India lose their fair reward of their work. The DMCA provides for such provision[484] with exceptions[485] to strike a balance between the two conflicting interest. Besides, the DMCA also exempts the Distant Education study copying[486].Whereas in India there is no such provisions. So we should have adjust our law this matters.

The analogue media gives protection to moral rights of author's as author's special right in Indian Copyright Act.[487] Therefore this provision can be extended to digital context for an effective protection of author's interest.

Necessity of fixing liability upon ISP

As a commercial entity, ISPs generally applying charge to general public or users for making available the information through Internet. Though the Indian Information Technology Act, 2000[488] gives immunity to the IPSs, there is no express provision relating to the liability of the service provider for infringement either in the Copyright or in the I. T. Act. The exemption of the liability of the service provider I.T Act[489]

---

[483] Ibid, Sec. 402.
[484] Ibid, Sec. 1201.
[485] Ibid, Sec. 1201 (a)-(g).
[486] DMCA, 1998, Sec. 403.
[487] Indian Copyright Act, 1957, Sec. 57.
[488] I.T. Act, 2000, Sec.79.
[489] Ibid.

never protect the legitimate interest of the copyright holder even if it is safeguarding the position of the service provider. Therefore addressing these type of issues, the best possible solution is to adopt a legislation like DMCA and OCILLA into India Copyright Act. Thus we can limit the liability of service providers.

There are provision for drafting of notice and the procedures after receiving the notice[490] and the service provider's responsibility to preserve the users[491] etc..... in the DMCA. Moreover if anybody misrepresented the copyright owner, the person should indemnify the service provider[492]. Then only the service provider will be exempted.

Another issue relating to the liability of service provider is that, anybody posted infringing material in the internet and provide a like to such materials and caching the material etc ...does not mentioned neither in the IT Act nor in the copyright Act, but there are specific provisions in the DMCA[493] regarding this matter, in order to exempt the service provider from liability. Thus the DMCA balance the interest of the Internet subscribers and copyright owner along with the service providers.

Indian copyright Act should also have to look into the concept of Electronic Rights Management[494] proposed by

---

[490] OCILLA, 1998, Sec. 512(g).
[491] Ibid, Sec. 512 (f).
[492] DMCA, 1998, Sec. 1201 (e).
[493] OCILLA, 1998, Sec. 512 (a)-(d)
[494] DMCA, 1998, Sec. 1202.

WCT 1996 which was adopted by ECD and DMCA. This provision encourage the author of a work to provide detailed information of such work and giving punishment to the violators.

All these changes are essential in India because a recent study proves that India has emerged as the fastest growing country of Internet users surpassing the growth rates of U.S, China, Japan in terms of netizens.[495] India had over 21 million Internet users, which will increase Infringement rate also.

---

[495] Business & Economy News Bureau, Indian netizens top growth chart, The New Indian Express, March 7, 2007.

ANNEXURE 1

The Information Technology Act, 2000

This is an Act to provide legal recognition for transactions carried out by means of electronic data interchange and other means of electronic communication, commonly referred to as "electronic commerce", which involve the use of alternatives to paper based methods of communication and storage of information, to facilitate electronic filing of documents with the Government agencies and further to amend the Indian Penal Code, the Indian Evidence Act, 1872, the Bankers Books Evidence Act, 1891 and the Reserve Bank of India Act, 1934 and for matters connected therewith or incidental thereto;

WHEREAS the General Assembly of the United Nations by resolution A/RES/51/ 162, dated 30th January 1997 has adopted the Model Law on Electronic Commerce adopted by the United Nations Commission on International Trade Law;

AND WHEREAS the said resolution recommends, inter alia, that all States give favourable consideration to the said Model Law when they enact or revise their laws, in view of the need for uniformity of the law applicable to alternatives to paper based methods of communication and storage of information;

AND WHEREAS it is considered necessary to give effect to the said resolution and to promote efficient delivery of Government services by means of reliable electronic records;

Chapter VII

Network Service Providers Not to Be Liable in Certain Cases

79. Network service providers not to be liable in certain cases.

For the removal of doubts, it is hereby declared that no person providing any service as a network service provider shall be liable under this Act, rules or regulations made thereunder for any third party information or data made available by him if he proves that the offence or contravention was committed without his knowledge or that he had exercised all due diligence to prevent the commission of such offence or contravention.

Explanation. -For the purposes of this section, -

(a) "Network service provider" means an intermediary;

(b) "Third party information" means any information dealt with by a network service provider in his capacity as an intermediary.